Christian Wholeness

Spiritual Direction for Today

by Jesse M. Trotter

Morehouse-Barlow Co., Inc. Wilton, Connecticut

To Marnie

Morehouse-Barlow Company, Inc.
78 Danbury Road
Wilton, Connecticut 06897

ISBN 0-8192-1294-6
Library of Congress Catalog Card Number 81-84718
Printed in the United States of America

Contents

Foreword

The characteristics of this book which seem to me to deserve special comment are threefold: its theology, its psychology and its integrity. There is also a significant conclusion which rises inevitably from these characteristics.

Dr. Trotter has spent most of his professional life as a teacher of theology—more precisely perhaps as an "apologist" (defender) of the Christian faith against the claims put forward by other views of the nature of reality and of human existence. He has therefore engaged and wrestled with the fundamental ideas of those thinkers who have been so formative for our culture, primarily Karl Marx, Sigmund Freud and Charles Darwin, as well as their twentieth century successors, the secularists, humanists, logical positivists and others.

This book is written with appreciation for the insights that come from these different world views (especially the Freudian) but from within a distinctly Christian theological framework. It is based upon the biblical and historical record of Christian experience, and most importantly as that experience is interpreted by the English theologian Frederick Denison Maurice and the Danish philosopher Søren Kierkegaard. They make a powerful team—the universal, all embracing thought of Maurice and the intense personal commitment of Kierkegaard—and provide Dr. Trotter with a secure, strong, theological perspective.

There is, therefore, first of all, an unwavering allegiance to the theology which rises from the biblical story: "the story of Deliverance and Covenant in the Old Testament and Deliverance in Christ and a new Covenant in him in the New Testament." It is the Gospel recorded and the Gospel lived by successive generations of Christians who by trusting Christ have shared with him through their own "dying to self" the power of his resurrection.

Along with his theological interpretation of the Gospel, Dr. Trotter brings also an appreciative perspective on the insights of contemporary psychiatry, particularly those of the Freudian school. Here he is particularly helpful in his realistic interpretation of aggression, sexuality and conscience, and the need for an honest view of one's own self-image.

Drawing upon his own experience in theological education, Dr. Trotter brings together his theological convictions and his psychiatric understanding. The seminary faculty he joined a generation ago was divided (as were most seminaries at that time) between the "theologians" and the "pastoral psychologists." In order to help bridge this division, Dr. Trotter underwent his own analysis for a number of years and then on a sabbatical leave undertook to bring together in a closer relationship the theological perspective of Frederick Denison Maurice and the psychological convictions of Sigmund Freud. The result provides the substance of this book.

Its overwhelming characteristic, therefore, is its integrity. It is not simply that the two views of the meaning of human existence—the theological and the psychological—are interwoven in a fresh and creative way, but that they have penetrated the heart and mind of one person. Dr. Trotter has lived the truth that is presented here.

Out of his own experiences as a Christian theologian who has gone through analysis and struggled with the meaning of his own pain and joy he writes with complete authenticity about the saving power of Christ. It is first-hand personal knowledge and it rings absolutely true. The key is that phrase which clearly has risen from the crucible of his own soul:

"To own and confess is Life,
To deny and disown is Death."

He has done what he bids us all do—he has chosen himself as he is, repentant before God, totally accountable to him. Therefore, more creative, more loving, more free. This book is one of those on spirituality which lives up to its title, *Christian Wholeness*, because it is written by a person who is himself becoming whole.

The conclusion which seems to me to rise inevitably from these three characteristics is that the church—but not denominational affiliation—is presented as an absolutely indispensable part of the Gospel, indeed is at the heart of the Gospel.

If you want to live "wholly" as a Christian, there is no way except in a loving (or trying to be loving) relationship with your fellow human beings and your fellow Christians who are themselves trying to be more "whole." What it means to be a Christian is inevitably discovered in the relationship one has with others who belong to the mystical Body of Christ. No matter how difficult that may be at times through membership in the institutional church, there seems to be no other way. The Gospel and the church belong together.

This book, then, is not only a defense of the Christian faith in the struggle with other world views in the contemporary world, though it is surely that, but it is also a moving testimony to the power of the living Christ in and through and with the other members of his Body. This is where true Christian wholeness is to be found.

vii

Christian Wholeness may become a classic. It surely speaks to the modern mind and spirit. It will in any case bring to any one who reads it a deeper understanding of his or her own nature and thus a deeper understanding of God's nature in Christ and of the power of his spirit for living more wholly.

John B. Coburn, Bishop
The Episcopal Diocese of Massachusetts

Preface

"The glory of God is a person who is fully human, fully alive." So wrote Irenaeus in the second century. Yet look about you. How many people seem to be busily contriving to stay half-well, half-alive? So we overwork, oversmoke, overeat, overdrink.

Wholeness has some fear in it for us. It threatens us in some way. To move forward on the path to wholeness is to experience a growing sense of a new inner freedom. Does the prospect of a genuine inner freedom make us anxious? "Anxiety is the dizziness of freedom," said Søren Kierkegaard.

We are the cleverest of all animals. If, in fact, wholeness does threaten us, we can run from wholeness, which also beckons us, in every possible direction. We can "run away forward" into work, backward in tranquilizers, upward into fantasy, downward into depression, sideways into evasion and avoidance. All to avoid the wholeness for which something else in us so hungrily longs.

The longing for wholeness finds many expressions:

"I feel so disordered at the center of my being."
"I feel so scattered and my life seems so scattered."
"I think things would go better with me if I knew what to believe."

"I am carrying around a great burden of self-dissatisfaction."
"I am too self-focussed. Somehow, and I don't know how, I
need to break free from myself."

As in all past ages, so in these days also, the longing for
wholeness is in part a longing for spiritual guidance and
spiritual direction. Spiritual direction, as defined here, is
the art of guiding a person, oneself or another, toward
wholeness. This book, however, is not a "how to" manual in
spiritual direction, replete with questions and answers, like
a hip-pocket edition on casuistry. A person with a caring
heart, whether ordained or not, will know what to say and
do in the one-to-one context of spiritual direction when
adequately instructed in spirituality. Concrete suggestions
for seeking wholeness and for spiritual direction are by no
means excluded from these pages. Nonetheless, instruction
in spirituality is our primary task, and for the following
excellent reason.

Spirituality is the matrix in which wholeness originates
and develops. Spirituality, or the spiritual life, encompasses
one's relationship to God, neighbor and self. The spiritual
life, when understood in such broad scope, might be too
much for us, too vague and mystifying, were it not for the
one ever-present focal point of reference and attention,
namely, God the Holy Spirit. The Holy Spirit, the Lord and
Giver of life, is the generating and nurturing power of
wholeness. How the Holy Spirit relates to the human spirit
is therefore a compelling concern throughout this book.

A reader has the right to know the orientation of the writer
and the influences which have shaped his thinking. I owe
much, indeed more than I can ever repay, to my own faith-
community, the Episcopal Church. Despite the fact that he
lived a hundred years ago, my chief "companion and
teacher" along the way, as well as a subject of serious study
for many years, is Frederick Denison Maurice (1805-1872).
In my judgment, he is the leading theologian in the Church
of England in the modern period. Maurice as a theologian is
remarkable for the fact that his rhetoric matched his

experience; his experience matched his rhetoric. His life and thought were all of a piece. He was a whole person.

Decisive for my life (and for this book also) is a particular congregation in Washington, D.C. I refer to The Church of the Saviour which has so forcefully and impressively brought home to me that word and sacrament, as well as individual daily disciplines and corporate mission, belong together. In each case, as with prophecy and liturgy, the one demands the other. Books about this remarkable parish are listed at the back of this book. Every one of these books is a milestone in the story of contemporary Christianity.

Professor Spencer McCallie Sr., Arthur Lee Kinsolving, Alexander C. Zabriskie, Gordon Cosby, Jenny Waelder Hall, M.D., and Irving and Marian Tallman Warner have all given me the experience which an early Quaker gratefully described: "I felt the evil within me weakened and the good raised up."

Part I of this book is entitled WHOLENESS and states the Biblical definition of wholeness, as well as definitions of the Holy Spirit and the human spirit. Part II is called SPIRIT AND STRUCTURE and deals with the human spirit in relation to the structure of the inner life as well as to the structure of the outer environment. Part III is concerned with THE NEW LIFE in Christ and with Christ. The parables of the Prodigal Son, the Pharisee and the Publican and the labourers in the Vineyard are revelatory of the Good News and are therefore given special attention in this section. Part IV on the JOURNEY TO WHOLENESS describes the stages of both the inward and the outward journeys, as well as the sources of the courage which will be needed.

The journey to wholeness now invites you. Recall the words of Goethe: "Whatever you can do or dream you can do—begin it."

Jesse M. Trotter

Alexandria, Virginia

Acknowledgements

The writer expresses his warmest appreciation to Dorothy Devers, Helene Spurrier, Jack Goodwin and John McEachern for reading the original "rough cut" and for their constructive suggestions, and to Bonnie Stratton for typing the final copy.

Part One
Wholeness

CHAPTER ONE
A Cry of Pain, A Cry of Joy

What God will do for those who offer Him
their weakness is beyond anything the strong
can do in their own strength.
                    Dorrit Pfau, 1979

The authority which defines the meaning of Christian wholeness is the Bible. If you do not acknowledge the intrinsic authority of the Scriptures as fully as this writer does, never mind. You may discover that the Bible possesses another kind of authority, namely, the authority of meaning, the meaning it can give to your life and to your search for wholeness. That scattered spirit of yours can be healed by the Power above all powers whose divine life the Bible reveals. Meaning and Power will give you not one but two handles on the authority of Scripture. These will suffice, quite apart from the intrinsic authority of the Bible when understood as the Word of God.

To define Christian wholeness in Biblical terms, and to describe what it means to seek wholeness, I shall briefly report three personal experiences. In sharing these experiences with you, I am, of course, using material with which I am most familiar. I make no apology for this. In the main body of the book, however, I shall minimize personal references.

Experience Number One

God spake these words and said: "Go through the center of the pain."

At twenty-two years of age I was teaching English and English literature in a university in Kyoto, Japan, having been given a two-year opportunity to do so by my alma mater, Amherst College. I quickly discovered the joy of teaching, my first love, and one which has given me the deepest satisfaction throughout my adult years. In Japan, I also encountered my first experience of crippling pain and helplessness.

Traveling during an academic vacation in China and Manchuria, I contracted a robust case of intestinal parasites. Lacking the immunity of a citizen of the area, I dropped in weight, with accelerating rapidity, from 160 pounds to 115 pounds. I was hospitalized for diagnosis and treatment. I suffered not as much from physical pain in the usual sense as from the pain which is peculiar to anemic weakness and the threat of helplessness. I was beset by the fear that I would continue to waste away and die. I prayed that I might recover and live, that I might become ordained as for some time I had wanted to be and that I might be given an opportunity to teach again. In that hospital I felt a degree of aloneness I had never known before.

Presently, as I prayed, I was not alone. There was a presence with me, a supporting and overarching presence. Actually, I heard no words. God is the supreme artist in nonverbal communication. Instead I was given a firm and quiet realization: "Go through the center of the pain. Do not deny it. Do not try to make an end run around it. Do not give up or give in to it. The only way ahead for you is to go through the center of the pain." That presence and that realization were one and the same reality. Of that I was convinced.

Eventually I was back in the classroom and glad once more to be teaching. I now experienced a different but corresponding realization: "Go through the center of the joy. Let yourself rejoice in what you are doing. Rejoice to the fullest."

The Lord our God is one. The God of pain and the God of joy are one God. Here was the hint of a mystery that has entranced my spirit and blessed my life from my youth to this day.

The report of a first-hand experience of God should surprise no one but of course it does.* We live in a wary and skeptical age. However, centuries of Christian experience have taught us that a personal experience of God is the birthright of every believer. We experience him as the Holy Spirit within ourselves, within our neighbors and especially we experience the real presence in the Holy Communion or Eucharist, as well as in a multitude of other ways.

Experience Number Two

God spake these words and said: "Foreclose on your childhood and your adolescence."

Here I might well substitute another heading: Theological Dog Fighting and Psychoanalysis. When thirty-seven years of age I was called to a theological seminary to teach that branch of theology which seeks to vindicate Christian truth vis-a-vis counter philosophies of this century: Marxism, naturalism and humanism, among others.

The faculty of the seminary at that time had fallen into

---

* On the personal experience of God, see Acts 17:28; Acts 26:12-19; II Timothy 1:12, 1:14; St. Luke 21:14-19.

two vaguely defined camps, "the theology people" versus "the psychiatry people." Naturally, the students tended to divide accordingly. The dog fighting was in the open, replete with a generous supply of barks and not a few bites.

My task was clear as well as intimidating. I must develop an "apologia" for theology as over against psychiatry. Unfortunately, I knew nothing about depth psychology. I therefore plunged into psychoanalysis, not reluctantly as one might have expected, but quite willingly. As the saying goes, "I had a problem." Both of my parents were rigidly shaped by a type of Calvinism which, I am sure, would have been an embarrassment to John Calvin. The kernel of my trouble, therefore, was a conscience which wore a Puritan hat and carried a loaded musket. My conscience was chronically trigger happy. The musket's target was a full array of desires, some good, some wayward and all mine. From college years I had often told my friends that I had a New England conscience and a southern chassis. At best, an angular combination. I had some homework of my own to do in psychoanalysis. I had the help of a cultured Viennese, physician and analyst, wise, highly trained and skillful. I needed all the help I could get from God, from her and from my understanding and long-suffering wife.

Five times a week, for several years, after the day's work was done, I commuted twenty-five miles (round-trip) to tangle with myself and with Dr. Sigmund Freud. I despised the whole thing at times, found release at others; I fought it, needed it; loathed it, welcomed it and finally came to that inevitable fork in the road. One path led to the scant but familiar comfort of continuing self-deceptions. The other path led from freedom to a greater freedom over a bridge of hard personal decisions. It was here that God spake these words and said: "Foreclose on your childhood and your adolescence." I chose that latter path.

I now had on my hands two doctrines of man: the Christian doctrine of Frederick Denison Maurice and the psychoanalytical doctrine of Freud. On a year's sabbatical I attended to the Yale Divinity School to relate the two in a private tutorial with Richard Niebuhr Sr., also a student of both men, as my mentor.

The human potential movement is perhaps Christianity's greatest rival in the modern world. Why? What is meant by the human potential movement? In the second quarter of this century, secular humanism (that is, belief in the self-sufficiency of man without God) was losing its vital signs. It was exhibiting symptoms of shock. Rigor mortis was a possibility. Then there came to the rescue of secular humanism the rich resources of depth psychology. The human potential movement is secular humanism rejuvenated by depth psychology.

There is no doubt whatever, at least in the minds of some of us who have benefited from its insights, that depth psychology has therapeutic power. A greater inner freedom is not to be scorned. The value of self-understanding, the invitation to participate in one's own life, to work upon one's own life as upon a material (Jaspers), to be self-responsible and to realize that we have ourselves as our task (Kierkegaard), that much can be done in self-actualization (Maslow), that ascendancy over the self is possible (Freud), that the need for self-kindness is undeniable (Jung), all deserve affirmation. Incidentally, a significant number of the above may be found in Freud's comprehensive thought and writing. However, not Freud but present day popular psychology has patched together a surrogate religion of dubious worth (as a religion) out of these and other valuable bits and pieces of psychology.

Popular psychology is often "bad" psychology. Like "bad" religion, it propagates detrimental teachings. The notion that instant anger instantly discharged makes for wholeness is a lie, one that is sometimes hard on family, co-workers and neighbors. Or the idea that an honest and truly open person should tell all—everything that is on the mind or comes to mind to anyone and everyone—is utter nonsense. Even a husband or a wife who "free-associates" at breakfast for three days running will wreck the family.

Psychoanalysis is a method of treatment; it is neither a philosophy nor a religion. Motivation for wholeness cannot be extracted from within it. Incentive must come from somewhere else, from suffering perhaps. Or incentive, motivation, inspiration to struggle for self-understanding may be found in true religion. To try to make up a religion out of depth psychology is to make inappropriate and unfair demands upon it, somewhat like trying to milk a fire hydrant.

To be sure I had to work through and appropriate within my emotional life (a very different thing from "intellectualistic" web-spinning) some hard, even brutal truths. These truths are really common sense but they often remain external to our emotional lives. In Greece there was a Pythagorean saying as long ago as 530 B.C.: "What follows learn to rule: the belly first, then sleep and lust and wrath."

All of which implies theologically that God holds us to self-responsibility and accountability to him. The Holy Spirit will help our human spirits but, fortified by his strength, we must resolve our inner conflicts and so overcome our personal anxieties. Evidently God does not displace or discourage human volition. On the contrary he encourages it. He counts on it. He frees it.

Reality, also, tells us that it is up to us as adults to gain the ascendancy over our own lives, that there is no significant growth without hard decisions and inner pain, that selfishness and wholeness cannot go together any more than selfishness and happiness can go together.

In short, as far as wholeness is concerned, the majority of persons need never learn even the vocabulary of psychoanalysis or that of any latter-day spin-off from the same, but every person needs, for the sake of her or his wholeness, to read, learn, mark and inwardly digest, that is, internalize the wisdom of the Scriptures.

To summarize and then to move on: In psychoanalysis I learned that I had to change inwardly. I went through the center of that pain in order to find the joy of a greater liberation. Once again the same, strange mystery: the God of pain is also the God of joy. I was subsequently to learn that true depth of that mystery.

Experience Number Three

God spake these words and said: "Live in the power of the cross and the resurrection of Jesus and you will be on the path that leads to wholeness."

When I was fifty-six years of age and busily at work as dean of a theological seminary, the absolutely unthinkable happened. My son John committed suicide at the age of twenty-two. From his earliest years a fun-loving, rambunctious lad, he seemed to be heading in all of the right directions. He spent five happy years at Choate School, playing on their undefeated football team in his senior year. His study at the Goethe Institute in Germany was followed by a scholarship year at All Hallows School in England. He chose to go to Princeton because of their style of football. He played freshman football but was not chosen to join the varsity squad in his sophomore year. Without football, he had to struggle to keep his weight down, even though he switched to rugby which he had learned to play in England.

His mother and I did not know that he had begun to use "speed" or amphetamine-type drugs to control his weight and had gradually developed a dependence. In November of his senior year he failed the Marine Corps physical examination because of high blood pressure, a consequence of the drugs as we were later to learn. Terminating the drugs abruptly, he forced himself to pass his mid-year examinations and then came home to us in an insidiously deep depression. He saw a psychiatrist for a month. Then, one April day as I entered the house at lunch time, a shot rang out. His mother and I rushed to the third floor. He had shot himself. He died in our arms. We were plunged into an agony of hours, of slow days and long nights, of weeks and months, and of years. Now, years later, the indescribable pain is gone. The sadness remains.

Our seminary community, our colleagues and students lovingly closed around us to comfort and support us. We unashamedly clung to them and to each other and, most of all, we clung to God. I now learned in depth of heart what Maurice had long since taught me intellectually that class-room notions, ideas, concepts of God are fragile things. You can fall through all such notions, ideas and concepts of God and you will fall into God. You will not fall through God into nothingness. There is a divine ground and that becomes the ground beneath your feet. You stand, and having done all, you stand because you are standing on the firm ground of God.

In my youth while in Japan the mystery of grace, the mystery of the one God of pain and of joy first came within my range of vision. For years I did not know that this mystery has a name, but it does. It is the paschal mystery: the experience in this life of a kind of cross-death followed by a kind of resurrection-life. "You were buried with Christ in baptism, in which you were also raised with him through faith in the working of God, who raised him from the dead" (Colossians 2:12).

Conclusion

The first chapter has presented in barest introductory

terms the paschal mystery and the Biblical definition of wholeness: Christian wholeness is living in the power of the cross and resurrection of Jesus.

To seek Christian wholeness is to learn more and more to live in the power of the cross and resurrection of Jesus.

How the Holy Spirit grasps the human spirit and enables one to learn how to do this and thus to become a whole person, one who dares to be "fully human, fully alive," is the path along which we shall travel in the chapters to follow.

Instead of running away from wholeness, we shall run to meet it.

CHAPTER TWO

Your Centered-spirit Is Spirit-led

The core of a person is his spirit; his spirit is
at the core and is the core.
                    Newton Gordon Cosby

Your spirit is another name for your personal center, for your innermost core, for what you mean when you say "I," for your adult ego. Your human spirit is intended to be self-directing, managing your capabilities and governing your activities.

Indeed, life lays upon you an unconditional demand that you become what you are, namely, a spirit that is free, self-managing, self-governing and reasonably, not rigidly, self-controlling. In the direction of "becoming what you are" lies part of what we mean by wholeness.

A Special Word about God and You

One autumn the four-year-old daughter of the Right Reverend Philip Alan Smith, the Episcopal Bishop of New Hampshire, was making her Halloween rounds dressed in a

10

witch's costume. Having knocked at the door of the first house on her itinerary, she found herself suddenly confronted by a man wagging his finger in her face saying playfully but tauntingly: "You're a witch!" "No," she protested proudly, "I'm not a witch. I'm a Smith!"

Although the analogy comes within a few millimeters of being inapt, so, according to the Scriptures, we have our source and origin in God. We are not witches. We are Smiths! God would have our spirits fortified by the knowledge that we come from him, the God of absolute power and infinite wisdom.

To know that Almighty God is the Father of our spirits should both give us courage and make us humble: Courage because of the sovereign majesty of the Creator and humility because of his limitless, loving mercy. By no means are courage and humility mutually exclusive. Both may be combined in a single spirit.

To know the nature of the God who is our source and origin, and to have the confidence this brings, should carry us well beyond the first milestones on the journey to wholeness.

A Special Word about Jesus and You

A respected teacher, Clifford Stanley, once said that never on this earth has there been a "self-made" man. Rather, he said, a person chooses a dominant influence to command his life. That influence makes him. He never makes himself. Whatever prevailing influence captures the spirit shapes the person.

Surely this is why Jesus in dealing with individuals always sought to discover what influence was controlling the center of the person. The story of the rich young ruler in Luke 18 is a case in point. His spirit was irretrievably locked into his wealth. Earlier Jesus said, "Where your treasure is, there will your heart be also " (Matthew 6:21). Jesus is saying that what is most treasured, most revered, shapes the heart, the personal center, the spirit and hence the whole person.

When we decide for God, that is, when we decide intentionally to belong to God, and make a mature, thoughtful commitment to the living Christ as the dominant influence which shall prevail over our spirits, we are taking a long step forward and an indispensable step toward wholeness.

A Special Word about the Holy Spirit and You

Whether we are speaking of the Holy Spirit or the human spirit, the word "spirit" carries the same definition. A spirit is a reality which has power over itself, is free, self-directing and self-managing. This means that God and man may meet Person to person, Spirit to spirit, even though they are radically different, as radically different as Creator and creature.

Stated bluntly, God the Holy Spirit does business with your personal center, with your adult, self-responsible and accountable human spirit. The Holy Spirit is the quickener, the awakener of the human spirit. A human being, this unique creature, does not need from the Holy Spirit impulses and impressions, needles and fixes which bypass the personal center. What he needs from the Holy Spirit, and time and again receives, is a new increment of life to awaken and energize his personal center. Thereby the individual may overcome his scatteredness and fragmentation and be supplied with a fresh sense of direction and of hope.

The above Special Words about God, Son and Holy Spirit affirm early in this book that they are not simply the constituent factors of a well-known religion and of a less well-known doctrine of the Trinity. They are the pillars of your personal being. They are the very ground of the wholeness you seek. What is more, they are on your side.

As I look over the last three sentences, I am content to say that sometimes scrambled metaphors are perhaps necessary to encompass the truth!

In Seeking Wholeness: The First Blind Alley

We are living in a century which has brought home to us in no uncertain terms the power of the good as well as the malignity of evil. Our age is knee-deep in blood. In this century we have killed or wounded in war eighty-seven million of our own kind, including those who have died in gas chambers and under torture but not counting those who have died from starvation. On the other hand the dynamic power of the good has given us Albert Schweitzer, Mahatma Ghandi, Martin Luther King and Mother Teresa of Calcutta. Their towering unselfishness is awesome, even terrifying, when compared with the egocentricity of our everyday concerns.

Dostoevsky, like Solzhenitsyn in our own day, was keenly aware that the forces of good and evil are too powerful for us either fully to comprehend or to control. The conflict of the kingdoms of good and evil persists in the world at large, in every society and in every human heart as well. Dostoevsky accuses Anglo-Saxon types of overlaying and obscuring the terrifying forces of good and evil with the more comfortable distinctions between right and wrong. A legalistic existence gives us an illusion of being in control. We thereby trap ourselves into centering our lives in moral striving rather than in God the Holy Spirit who alone can overcome the powers of evil in us and beyond us.

Distinctions between right and wrong are of course important and moral striving, as we shall see, has a significant place in life. However, as we shall also see, to center one's life in human striving is to invite impoverishment of spirit and loss of life, the very reverse of wholeness. To go this way is to enter a blind alley and many there be who find it.

In Seeking Wholeness: The Second Blind Alley

"God helps those who help themselves." When we lift the rough tarpaulin of Benjamin Franklin's aphorism, we find only the barest fragment of truth. Human initiative, originating an act, does of course have its place. Isle au Haut, an island several miles off the coast of Maine, has been known to be ice-bound in a very severe winter, with a sheet of ice stretching to the mainland. This always means dragging a sled over the ice for mail and supplies. A lobsterman walking toward the mainland with his sled in tow noted that the shore line seemed always and forever to be receding before him. "There was only one thing I could do," he said, "I had to move my legs and wait." Initiative, placing one foot in front of the other, was essential.

I inquired of one of my abler students why the quality of his work was not better. "Well," he said, "after dinner at night I don't find myself in the library." My mind reached back to the lobsterman on his long, freezing trek. I therefore suggested to the student that after dinner he point his course from the dormitory to the library, less than a hundred yards away, and then "just move your legs and wait." His work improved. Initiative helps. First, mine. Then, his. There is a whole realm of everyday existence wherein human initiative is indicated, as in going after the mail, groceries or a book. However, where wholeness and our relationship to God are concerned, God's initiative comes first. This the Bible makes repeatedly clear.

A cynical interpretation of "God helps those who help themselves" is Falstaffian: "Why, then the world's mine oyster, which I with sword will open." God becomes my assistant in finding the pearl.

To any degree whatsoever or in any sense whatever, to entertain the notion that God is exploitable by us is a second blind alley. The temptation to enter this blind alley is almost irresistible because of our deep longing to have things happen our way and for everything to turn out all right in the end, without cross and without care.

The fragment of truth in Franklin's aphorism lies here: We may take the initiative in responding to God's initiative. "We love (him) because he first loved us" (I John 4:19). To be sensitively contemporary, we need a veritable corkscrew of words to open the wine bottle, as Daniel Jenkins comments: "God responds to our response to his initiative."

Summary and Transition

To be "spirit-centered" has a twofold meaning. As individuals our personal center is our spirit. We constantly need recentering. To consolidate our personal centers is a necessity if we are to overcome scatteredness and fragmentation. In this task the Holy Spirit is the center of reference for our personal center. He is our lodestar. He is our ally and helper, our inner guide and strengthener, in recentering our lives.

Our personhood finds its center in our human spirit. Our human spirit finds its center in the Holy Spirit.

> *Speak to Him for He hears*
> *And Spirit with spirit can meet.*
> *Closer is He than breathing*
> *And nearer than hands and feet.*
> *Alfred Lord Tennyson*

Every human spirit lives in two environments. We quite easily recognize that we live in an outer environment, the world of physical nature, extending into the unthinkable vastness of outer space. We are not as much at ease when

seriously reflecting upon our inner space. Perhaps you are
not as familiar as you might be with the inner components of
personality in the midst of which your spirit exists. There is
a whole congress of components surrounding your core,
your personal center—all contained within the inner
environment.

Part Two
Spirit and Structure

CHAPTER THREE
The Inner Environment

*No man can bear the burden of himself who
does not bow down before something greater
than himself.*

Dostoevsky

To examine the main components of your personality
enables you to see what it means for your spirit to preside
over the Congress of the Interior. Your aggression, your sexuality, your conscience and your self-image constitute what
may be called your Congress of the Interior. To understand
this inner environment of your spirit is to take another step in
the direction of wholeness.

After all, the same components which make for mental
and spiritual health and wholeness also make for mental
and emotional illness. How important, therefore, that we
have knowledge of them.

Aggression

*Daughter Marian, thee must not bite thy sister
Emalea. Thee must not leave thy tooth in her
arm.*

A Quaker Father

17

The words of the Quaker father were certainly cataclys-
mic in a family of Quaker descent, and perhaps they were
apocryphal. The indicated facts, however, are straightforward history. Six-year-old Marian, overwhelmed by her
anger at the teasing and other depredations of eight-year-old
sister Emmie, sprang from her launching pad one day on a
trajectory which intersected with her sister's upper arm.
The attacker, using a weapon provided by nature, clamped
her mandibles on her sister's tender flesh. Unhappily, only
one wobbly baby tooth remained in the central arsenal. At
point of impact, the tooth separated from the first stage of
the living rocket, to find lodgement for a time in her sister's
upper arm. In due course the implant was rejected by the
new host as a foreign body, fell back to earth and was lost in
the melee.

Had the younger sister submitted passively to the older
sister's teasing, she might have grown up to be a shy,
retiring and silent woman. She did not and she is not,
although she is no longer impelled by cannibalistic regres-
sions. Her aggression was, and is, a beneficial resource for
her spirit.

Aggression is the first drive or resource to be observed in
the newborn infant. The louder he howls, the more angrily
he bellows as he makes his first appearance in the world, the
more the proud father, often an onlooker in these days,
inwardly cheers. The power of the infant's hue and cry
when he is hungry and the energetic bent of his nursing are
considered promising. Inborn aggression is indeed a
resource from (as well as for) our first breath.

A committee gathers to interview a young person who is
seeking admission to the ordained ministry. A layman, new
on the committee, addressed the first question to the
chairman of the admissions committee, the dean of the
school, "What do you look for in these applicants?" The dean
replied, "Sooner or later I want to find out whether an

applicant has any fight in him or in her." The layman instinctively understood.

The capacity to strive, to struggle, to work, to fight for chosen goals is necessary to every profession and in every job. Aggression, hostility, anger, hatred are interchangeable terms as far as their inner meanings are concerned. In fact they share a common inner meaning: raw biologically-rooted energy, the power to move, to strive, to act, to do, to work, to fight. Of course people differ in their natural drive endowments. Some persons, most persons in fact, are overdetermined and oversupplied with aggression; some are undersupplied.

An abundant supply of aggressive drive is indeed a most useful tool of the human spirit. Some Christian interpretations to the contrary, possessing a capacity for aggression and anger is not a sin. The human spirit, the personal center, whether of a man or a woman, has the responsibility of admitting to himself or herself anger when present and of deploying and using aggression constructively. Your aggression poses two dangers for you. In the first place, you may deny the presence of angry feelings, feel guilty about them and then "take it out on yourself" for having them. You may "diesel" after you have turned off the ignition until you inwardly rattle yourself loose and out of sorts.

The other danger is that, even as an adult, you may not have developed in this permissive society sufficient self-control to manage your temper, your rage, your aggression. Then others will shun you or will "take it out on you" by counteraggressions of their own. We shall pick up on this important matter in Chapter 6.

Sexuality

We know each other's nakedness better than we know each other.

Anonymous (c. 1965)

Your spirit does not have an easy role in relation to your aggression or in relation to your sexuality. However, properly understood, they both belong to the Security Forces of your spirit; both aggression and sexuality are important members of the Congress of the Interior.

As with aggression, so with sexuality, the human dilemma appears to be one of overcontrol or undercontrol. An era of Puritanical overcontrol seems always to be followed by a period of license in which "all is permitted." We are now living in an "all is permitted" age.

We are living in a society where, as Joan Didion says about San Bernardino, "it is easy to misplace the future and start looking for it in bed." We are rediscovering the power of casual and "quickie" sex to reduce personal integration, to provoke self-alienation and to fracture family solidarity.

On the other hand, unlived and unsublimated sexuality in the individual can be the cause of a troublesome, often unidentified anxiety. There can be no wholeness for the human being unless both aggression and sexuality are accepted, integrated into the personality and given places of high honor in the self-respect of the human person.

Fortunately there are resources both within the individual's inner environment and in the transcendent outer environment which enable the human spirit to manage creatively both his aggression and his sexuality, as we shall see in Chapter 6.

Conscience

It is easier to relax a strict conscience than it is to restrict a lax conscience.
                              Jenny Waelder Hall

Conscience is still another component of the human personality. A human being without a conscience is something less than human. The conscience back-stops the personal center, guides the spirit, warns a person when his integrity is threatened and is essential to wholeness.

The enormous value of the conscience to civilized man has often induced religion erroneously to equate the conscience with some kind of divine power. "The voice of conscience is the voice of God." How much unnecessary inner suffering and agony of heart and just plain unhappiness have been caused by this falsehood is beyond reckoning.

The Christian religion has given the conscience close and persistent attention down the centuries. The Church has known how to relieve "the pain of conscience" by formal confession and the sacrament of penance. However, not until the work of Freud have we understood the extent to which the conscience is of social origin.

Freud describes the conscience as a parental institution within the mind which leads us to judge ourselves and to treat ourselves exactly the way our parents judged us and treated us as children. Quite literally we internalize those earliest external authorities, our parents, and other early educators.

Sophie Clippard, a gifted teacher of art to kindergarten and first grade pupils, engaged in an interesting experiment. She asked her pupils to draw pictures of their own fathers and mothers with themselves standing near them. A composite of her pupils' work is shown in Figure 1.

An examination of the drawing will immediately tell you that the origin of the expression "the eye of conscience" is father's critical eye. In the traditional family the father represents "the law," the laws of society. The father stands for society's limits and prohibitions.

Mothers in the midst of their young broods and often on the verge of helplessness in the face of boisterous, nonstop activity, not to mention fights and brawls, are driven at times to yell at their children. To the children their mothers appear to be yelling out of large, square mouths which, bless all mothers, they probably are. The "voice of conscience" is not always a "still small voice." In the modern family the mother also proclaims the law, as well as being a court of appeal.

Figure 1
Initial Sources of the Conscience
(a composite of drawings by five and six year olds)

As parents and combinations of parents are infinitely varied, so with consciences. Parents may be firm and reasonable in necessary disciplines and restrictions. They may be overly strict and unreasonable. Some parents are downright cruel and sadistic.

The human spirit will treat itself accordingly. You have known persons who were self-belittling, always putting themselves down. The agony-producing conscience of Martin Luther was unbearable. He turned to God for grace and help with his own conscience and he was not disappointed.

Many observers have noted that the conscience is the only component of the human personality which is soluble in alcohol. A drink helps a person "to get himself off his own back." For a time he feels a bit lighter. However as a chronic remedy, alcohol, by repeatedly dissolving the conscience, cripples the spirit. When we drink too much, we surprise even ourselves by what we do. The conscience passes out before we pass out.

Far more disastrous in many ways than a cruel conscience is a poorly formed, overly permissive conscience. Such a conscience has frequently been compared to Swiss cheese. Large holes are everywhere present, unfilled from infancy by overindulgent parents.

The personal center, lacking a firm conscience, has nothing to grow strong "against." There are no high claims with which the developing spirit must come to terms. Of course, if the claims are impossibly high, the adolescent at the time of his natural and necessary rebellion may reject them altogether. On the other hand, if the claims are minimal, the spirit remains "unjelled" and flabby.

One parent, considering herself very modern and sophisticated, commented on her fourteen-year-old daughter, Susie, who was taking full advantage of this "all is permitted" age. "Oh, I don't worry about Susie. When she's eighteen, I'll send her to an analyst." No comment could be more naive. An analyst can work only with and through Susie's personal center and by eighteen years of age Susie's spirit may be tapioca. A sixteen-year-old Roman Catholic girl was brought to an analyst of teenagers who said something to this effect: "What a relief! There is some spirit and structure in this girl with which I can work."

A spiritual task of superhuman proportions awaits the individual who must fill in the holes in a Swiss cheese conscience, if such a conscience is his fate. This is perhaps the hardest work he will ever be called upon to do on the journey to wholeness. To replace infidelity with fidelity in marriage, dishonesty with honesty in business, unfairness to students with fairness as a teacher, the priest's pride of life with humility, being fair and just to those we dislike instead of conveniently ignoring them—one or more may be indicated.

However difficult the task, many Christian individuals have demonstrated that it can be done. Here in this context specifically we may see that spirituality is the matrix of wholeness and that there can be no spirituality without discipline, that is, self-discipline. In this task, as in many others, the Holy Spirit is the ally and helper of the human spirit. The path to wholeness summons us to the practice of prayer without which the required transformation of the conscience is impossible. In Chapter 7 we shall explore prayer further.

The conscience embodies the law. The law forms the spirit. Grace redeems it. Grace enables us to retrain an inadequate conscience. Grace also enables us to forgive ourselves, as God forgives us, when our consciences condemn us. Reflective prayer and meditation can help us whether our consciences are too rigid or are underdeveloped. Fortunate are those who have firm, mature consciences with which they can cultivate friendly relations, even when their consciences are somewhat too rigid. Hence the words placed at the beginning of this section: "It is easier to relax a strict conscience that it is to restrict a lax conscience."

The Self Image

Finding out what you want to be is the main struggle.

Rufus Jones

The conscience has a twin: the self-image. The conscience speaks to us chiefly in negative terms and, if harsh in nature, lays upon us "the lash of the ought." The self-image speaks in positive terms, represents the kind of person we would like to be, the qualities we admire and seek to incorporate, the values we have chosen to serve. To clarify our goals in life is to establish our self-image and, in so doing, our self-identity as well.

We can better understand both the adolescent and ourselves if we pause to examine the source and foundation of every person's self-image. Once again, as with the conscience, the self-image derives in the first instance from father and mother.

Even ridiculing, sarcastic parents are at times happy and smiling (see Figure 2). Children in their early years typically wish to be like their parents, a boy like his father, a girl like her mother. These earliest identifications constitute the bottom layer of the self-image. Later other admired persons, teachers and coaches, contribute additional layers of the self-image.

The adolescent problem—and the reason adolescence is such a difficult stage in human experience—is the necessity the young person faces: he must move forward from his parents' image of what they want him to be to his own chosen self-image.

Not just in passing but with utmost seriousness we must note that there has been a shift of the continental plates in the culture of Europe and America. A basic change has taken place in the last twenty-five or thirty years. The rising generations experience life differently from the middle aged and older generations. We must not allow the phrase "the generation gap" or the expression "there's always been a generation gap" to obscure the gravity of what has, and is, taking place. I refer to the fact that the nature of inner conflicts has changed, due largely to the affluence of the peoples of the west, or rather, the majority of these peoples. Even the poor of the west are well off compared with the world's poor.

Figure 2
Initial Sources of the Self-Image
(a composite of drawings by five and six year olds)

Inevitably inner conflicts are experienced by every human being. Now, however, we cannot understand the age in which we live unless we distinguish between vertical and horizontal conflicts. Middle aged and older persons of today have known and still know the experience of vertical conflicts, which is to say, conflicts between duty and desires, between conscience and physical drives, sometimes spatially (and not too appropriately) referred to as conflicts between the "higher centers" of the personality (conscience and reason) and the "lower centers" (sexuality and aggression).

Many younger persons in their teens, twenties and even thirties, through no fault of their own, have been given less opportunity to strengthen their personal centers. They have experienced comforts and a measure of affluence never before known in the world except by a very small minority. They experience a longer economic and emotional dependence on their parents (in some cases denying it the more vehemently). Their thrust for independence in adolescence and as they seek to cross the threshold into adult life is exaggerated in direct proportion to the earlier, greater dependence. Their inner conflicts which are experienced as "strung-out-in-time" from childhood to adulthood I call horizontal conflicts to distinguish them from the vertical conflicts mentioned above. Immediately, we must note that most individuals experience some measure of both types of inner conflict, but it is the accent on one rather than the other which makes the critical difference to the parents and their offspring of today.

Someone attempting to offer spiritual direction to an individual stuck in the morass of a dependency-independency conflict may be of help by asking: "What is your self-image?" "What do you want to be?" "What do you want to do?" How easy to state these questions. How difficult for the hearer to work through them!

God is willing and able to help us. We need not suffer the torture of our conflicts alone. He sends his Spirit to strengthen and guide the human spirit in its journey through conflicts toward wholeness.

After goals are clarified and commitments are made, when all the interior components are pulling together in the service of known objectives, the human spirit is moving toward wholeness. How easy to state. How difficult to achieve at best, and especially if we try to go it alone. For the spirit experiences a certain powerlessness which has cultural causes (as examples: affluence and permissiveness). The human spirit also suffers from the consequences of the Fall, resulting in a far more serious kind of powerlessness, a subject which will come before us in the next chapter.

CHAPTER FOUR

The Outer Environment

*God in whom we live and move and have
our being.*

Book of Acts (17:28)

Man belongs to the total environment. He is a little lower than the angels, and he is of the earth, earthy. He is a laminated creature, somewhat (but only somewhat!) like plywood. In the evolutionary process he was, as it were, built up layer by layer.

Nicolai Hartmann*, the German philosopher, points out that each of us is composed of inorganic materials, minerals, for example, and other chemicals. After the cremation of a single human body, the residue is really quite small. This naturalistic basis of our life is that indispensable bottom layer.

The second layer, next to the bottom one, is the organic, animal layer. We are all card-carrying members of the animal kingdom. The same sexuality and aggression which

---

*Vide Nicolai Hartmann, *The New Ways in Ontology* (Chicago: Henry Regnery, 1953).

gave survival power to the ruling mammalian dynasty finally placed, for good or ill, the fate of all mammals and the good earth as well in the hands of the current ruling species, the human race.

The third layer is the psychic life which is found in man and, in rudimentary form, in some of the higher vertebrates. Consciousness and self-awareness, factors in the psyche, represent features of life not too well understood. For thousands and thousands of years mammals existed which possessed psychic life before the spirit, the fourth "layer" and the most remarkable of all life realities, emerged to over top psychic life.

That Hartmann uses the word spirit to designate the summit and culmination of the evolutionary process is all the more remarkable when we consider that he is a secularist, lacking belief in a transcendent Spirit. He finds the human spirit empirically present, a newcomer on the earth. "So God created man. . . . ." (Genesis 1:27).

Hartmann notes the dependence of the human spirit upon all three of the lower layers, consciousness, self-awareness and the necessary defense mechanisms of the psychic layer; the biological, animal layer; the simple but intricately inter-related chemical properties; all three layers support the spirit.

The human spirit is indeed utterly dependent upon every one of the lower layers. We are part of the total environment, related to the good earth beneath us and to transcendent Spirit above us.

In the stratified structure of the world the lowest layer, consisting of inorganic substances, in one sense is the strongest. In another sense the spirit is the strongest.

The lowest inorganic layer is the least vulnerable to death and destruction. As already indicated, our bodies are biodegradable. The chemicals are recycled. Imagination permits me to fancy that my skeletal frame is now making more or less constructive use of calcium, carbon, copper and other inorganic oddments recycled from a mongoose or perchance an opossum. I like being related to the other animals, sharing alike, for a time at least, the chemical substances of the good earth.

On the other hand, the spirit is the strongest layer, in spite of its dependence on the lower layers. The spirit is the knowing, planning and executive power of the total organism.

The spirit is endowed with a capacity to understand and correct many of the foes of mind and body: chemical imbalances, bodily diseases, psychic distortions. Thanks to modern science we know much already and we are learning more all the time. Even when crippled and handicapped, a person can find wholeness. Such is the power of the spirit. I have known truly whole persons who were blind or confined to canes, crutches, wheelchairs or to their beds. It is as though, from the beginning, God has determined that you shall not be a loser.

In summary we are part of the world, bone of its bone.

Death is not to be denied, "pan-cake" it as we will. We really die, spirit and all. Nor is the oblivion of death to be feared. Even in the grave you belong to him and he watches over you. Resurrection will occur. The prospect of death does not stand in the way of wholeness. Death can be integrated into our life, as we shall presently see.

The greatest hindrance to wholeness does not come from the lower layers of being or from the fact that death awaits us. The mortal enemy of wholeness is sin. Sin afflicts the spirit itself. The human spirit becomes its own worst enemy. How this came about is the subject to which we now turn.

The Image of God

The Bible proclaims three principal characteristics of

Almighty God. The divine Power who is the source of all things is creative, loving and free.

The creative nature of God is incorporated in one of the most familiar of all of our names for God: God the Creator. The world together with all that is in it, and even more, the miraculous universe of which it is a part, bear testimony to God's creative nature and power.

Love is understood to be God's motive in his creation, a love which is further understood to be of a personal nature. In the words of a liturgy, He has made his love known to us "in the calling of Israel, in the words of the prophets, and, above all, in Jesus his Son." God's love found expression in the redeemer who was "God of God, Light of Light, Very God of Very God" and who for us and our salvation came and was made man. God's love has come to us in the founding of the Church, in the designation of the apostles, in the Scriptures and in the Sacraments, in his judgment and in his grace down the centuries to this day. Love is God's inner-most nature.

The mystery of the Holy Spirit cannot be captured or contained in a definition, as we have already noted. However, a single word that comes closest to its inner meaning is the word "freedom." "Spirit" and "freedom" may be used interchangeably in many contexts. When the Holy Spirit brings a new increment of life to the human spirit, that gift always brings an awareness of being set free. The Holy Spirit is the Lord and Giver of Life. The Spirit may also be called the Liberator. "Where the Spirit of the Lord is, there is freedom" (II Corinthians 3:17).

The ancient doctrine of the Trinity affirms the image of God. God is creative, loving and free.

The Image of Man

What does it mean in this world here and now that you

are made in the image of God, as Genesis declares? It means that God created you in your essential nature to be creative, loving and free.

You experience yourself as most real, and as most yourself, when you are being creative in your vocation or in your avocation. Paradoxically, you lose yourself most completely, break free from yourself most fully and are least aware of yourself when you are being creative. On the other hand, unused creativity makes one self-preoccupied, unstrung and restless. How often mental depression is the ache of a neglected and perhaps unidentified gift. It is costly business to disown one's essential nature.

The wonder and grandeur of human nature is never more evident than when a person, in an act of total self-giving love "lays down his life for his friends," as Jesus said and as he did. Similarly, made in God's image, you are most the person you were created to be, and essentially are, when you are giving and receiving love, within the family, the school, the community, the nation, the world. Jesus set no geographical limits.

A telling illustration of love at work may be found in the way a teacher sees himself and goes about his work. If he makes a point of knowing his students well enough to discover their strengths and weaknesses and then builds on their strengths, love and appreciation are at work. On the other hand, if he looks only for weaknesses, he may, perhaps unwittingly, augment his own conceit and self-righteousness, but he will not elicit a self-confidence in the student which will enable the student to increase his strengths and to grapple with his own weaknesses.

The teacher who judges his student in terms of the best that is in him will be the happier because he is exercising his capacity to love. To probe for weaknesses and offer one's services chiefly as a pedagogical repair man will perhaps free the teacher to engross himself totally in exciting ideas, but he will also accumulate much unlived life as his capacity to love is ignored or disowned. Many a contemporary teacher will label what I am now writing as maudlin rot and, as one college teacher told me, as "fatuous character stuff." (Let such skeptics learn of Abraham Flexner's philosophy of education, of his early work as a secondary school teacher and of his later work in reforming medical education in America). These critics might well address themselves to the question of why much education in America has become an empty enterprise. Can computers, either the biped variety or the immovable type, make up what is lacking?

In his essential nature man is not only creative and loving. He is a free being. He was created so to be. His spirit possesses freedom and acts in freedom. Freedom is experienced in the wake of a decision, of a deed long postponed but finally done, of an act of confession, or after initiating a reconciliation. We seem most real to ourselves, and sometimes to others, when we are most free.

However, we are gripped with a radical pity for mankind, and with an uncanny terror, when we contemplate the human condition in terms of man's capacity to fall into the opposite of his essential nature. When he falls into his opposite, he can be demonic. His essential nature, that of being creative, loving and free, presents us with an undistorted humanity we hardly recognize, either in ourselves or in others. If his essential nature were the whole story, we would not have to seek wholeness. We would have it.

The Fall—A Likely Story

The Biblical story of the Fall is more than a likely story. It is a truth-full story. Certain kinds of truth can be communicated only in parables, stories, sagas. How paltry and prosaic are all definitions of courage, heroism, friendship, love, dread, hope, agony of heart, betrayal of others, self-betrayal. The meaning of these realities enters the mind through the portal of the imagination. The imagination needs more than a flat definition to enliven and inform the mind. It needs a story or a legend or a saga.

The Fall is the legendary and truth-laden story of man on this earth, created to live in harmony with God, with his neighbor, and with himself. He was fashioned, as we have seen, in the image of God, to be creative, loving and free. In the Fall he became the opposite of himself. He became a conflicted being, with his spirit caught between fierce, opposing impulses. His spirit was and is torn between the need to create and the need to destroy, the need for freedom and a longing for complete and irresponsible abandonment, the need to love unselfishly and the need for self-glorification. When we allow the story of the Fall to throw light on the human condition, on the human contradiction, on man as the opposite of himself, the illumination is as telling in the twentieth century as it was in the first.

Who is not shocked by the sadism of much of the world's cruelty. The aggressive sadism exhibited daily in the life of our country and of the world, in homicides and in killing just for the sake of killing? Or the sexual-aggressive sadism exposed in child abuse and in battered wives?

If we will remove our Anglo-Saxon blinders which seem to be almost of genetic origin, we may look into the murky depths of our dark side. The cold, unacceptable truth is that "deep-down-under" in every human person there is a seducer and a killer. How we recoil from that fact! We escape the truth by exaggerating it. You may be prone to say, "The writer is telling me that every person is a seducer and a killer—how absurd!" Such a statement is absurd. In every person there is a seducer and a killer. Early in life the hatch is dogged down and shut tight over this unwelcome truth. It is simpler, less frightening simply to deny this ugly truth about ourselves.

We see the seducers and killers in other persons clearly enough as we read and examine newspapers and magazines, novels and TV shows. Exploiters of the human condition make millions of dollars by reporting, writing about, and by big screen showings of what happens when the seducers and killers break through the controls and defenses of the impoverished human spirit. Something in us is willing freely to part with our money to see the worst, hidden in ourselves, acted out by others.

To exaggerate the importance to our self-understanding, as a race and as individuals, of the truth conveyed by the doctrine of the Fall is almost impossible. How readily and with what ease do we become the opposite of ourselves and with what disastrous consequences.

How otherwise can we understand our human addiction to war? As far back as anthropologists can trace in history, and in prehistory for that matter, we have been war-aholics. Beneath the foundation walls of a theological seminary chapel, of all places, was recently found the stone head of a prehistoric battle axe. The stone was hard enough to break hostile craniums but too soft for any other viable (sic) purpose. Skulls with holes in the head to correspond have also been found in Stone Age excavations. In our fallen natures we can become killers, viciously destructive, prototype vandals, in short, predators. Neighbors prey upon neighbors, as predators upon predators. Basic human nature has not changed.

Our magnificent creativity has provided us with the means of a technological warfare which in our fallenness we cannot handle. Our peril is not greater than we know. We know the danger. The so-called superpowers are also the superfallen, simply because we have such dizzy and dizzying heights from which to fall. Reality mandates that we try for a standoff, a stalemate, matching gun for gun, bullet for bullet, bomb for bomb. Yet we doubt. We tremble. We know the awesome truth of the Fall.

Without this truth of the Fall how can we even understand our conduct in our own homes? Why do we hurt those whom we love the most? Hate is the flipside of love. Note how instantaneous the flip can be. The desire to hurt a loved one is the Fall-side of a willingness to die for that same loved one. We are conflicted beings.

In these deepest matters psychiatry has little to offer. A not uncommon cause of death among psychiatrists is suicide. What is suicide but the turning of a killing hatred against oneself, perhaps as a substitute for the real object of the suicide's murderous anger? Such is our universal need to be healed and made whole by a power greater than ourselves.

Especially difficult to face is the presence in the human spirit of a need to hate. Strange that facing this particular fact is so difficult. Every section of our country has one or more minority or ethnic groups for the majority to hate. Where none exists, one is invented.

Maurice acknowledged his need to hate and put it constructively to work. He hated the unequal treatment of women in his country and founded the first women's college in Great Britain. He hated social injustice and became the father of the British Cooperative Movement. He hated ignorance and founded night classes for factory workers in a country which did not offer universal education. There are constructive uses even for hate when the spirit is living in the power of the cross and resurrection and has been healed and made whole.

Most fateful for the human spirit is man's fall from loving God and his neighbor into self-glorification. As we have already noted, love is the very nature of God. Man, made in his image, is flawed at the point of his nearest kinship to God, namely, in his capacity to love. Self-glorification, our fall into overweening self-love, affects all of the components of the personality: self-centered and self-serving use is made of conscience (rationalization), the self-image (pretentiousness), sexuality (self-gratification only), and aggression (selfish power-seeking).

The disposition to separate oneself from one's essential self, from one's neighbor and from God is precisely the meaning of sin. The contraction and impoverishment of the human spirit as well as the enhanced sinfulness of the human spirit are the chief consequences of the Fall.

The human spirit does indeed become its own worst enemy. Our poverty—the impoverishment of our spirits, which are conflicted and fragmented, alienated from God, from our neighbors and from ourselves, and therefore so very much in need of wholeness—is why Christ came.

He came to restore us to our essential selves. He came to make us whole.

Part Three
The New Life

CHAPTER FIVE

Faith-Union with Christ

As both cause and content of this new reality (The New Life), Paul names Christ the Lord, and he is never tired of emphasizing again and again what supreme happiness, freedom, and strength this life "in Christ" bestows, and of proclaiming to Christians . . .the granting of the new life by divine grace.*

Martin Dibelius

Paul, known in the earlier part of his life as Saul, is a valuable guide to all who seek wholeness, especially to all of us who are present-day seekers.

Saul of Tarsus was a favored son of Judaism. He was a Pharisee of the Pharisees, the most earnest and respected of all the people of Israel. Rabbinically trained, he was equipped with a first-rate education in the Sacred Writings of his people. In addition, he had been reared in a colony of Jews in Tarsus, a city near the southern shores of present-day

---

*Martin Dibelius, Paul (Philadelphia: The Westminster Press, 1966), p. 64.

Turkey, in those days a city of Greek culture but under
Roman rule. More than any of the apostles, he knew Gentiles,
their mind-set, their customs and their gods. Tarsus-born,
he was a Roman citizen. And God needed him and had
plans for him. In fact, God intervened in the life of Saul of
Tarsus shortly after the crucifixion of Jesus, very possibly in
the year 34 A.D.

Saul had a temperament of fire, precisely the right individual for the Pharisees to let loose upon the troublesome
clique of Jesus' disciples who were frequenting the syna-
gogues of Jerusalem and being very outspoken in their
proclamation that Jesus of Nazareth, crucified and risen,
was the Messiah. Absurd, blasphemous, scandalous: The
Messiah, the long expected one, chosen of God victoriously
to lead and save his people, certainly could not have come
out of Galilee, an area populated by many despised "for-
eigners," as well as by poor artisans, farmers and fisherfolk.

The "Galilean" heretics were also perpetrating their
mischief in outlying villages and towns. The Pharisees of
Jerusalem authorized Saul of Tarsus to track them down
and to bring them as captives to Jerusalem. Of necessity,
therefore, he spent much time with them. In the power of
the Spirit they bore their "testimonium" to him. Saul of
Tarsus, when he allowed himself to listen to them, may have
thought that he was only collecting evidence to use against
them. In fact, he was inviting his own downfall.

The captives, as they were being herded to Jerusalem,
repeated to Saul many times over the parables of Jesus,
especially those parables which challenged the Pharisees'
traditional understanding of God.

Vast courage was needed by those captives who told him
the parable of the father who had two sons. The older son
was endlessly loyal to his father, punctilious to the letter in
obeying his father's instructions as they daily worked on the
family's farm. The younger son was recalcitrant, a free

spirit. He wanted distance between himself and his father and of course from his Jewish mother, and especially from that brother.

Pocketing his patrimony which his father generously did not hide or withhold from him, he set out for a distant country notorious for its countless and elaborate pleasure spots. In such a country, whores were in high demand, could name their own stipends, and, one may surmise, on a nightly basis were extraordinarily expensive. The farmer's son was soon penniless. He slept where he could hide and ate out of garbage pits, as our street people do in our cities today.

Early one morning I saw a prodigal son eating his breakfast out of a garbage can which had been placed alongside the ramp leading up to the west side highway in New York. He was finishing the driblets remaining in two Coke cans and eating the discarded portion of a fly-laden hot dog.

In comparable desperation the Hebrew lad in our story turned homeward and to his father. He confessed the sin of his separation and of his moral abandonment to his loving, forgiving and joyful father. His father could not contain himself. He laid on a feast of feasts. His lost son had come to himself and was home again which was all that mattered.

The older son was peeved, disgruntled, resentful, hating his father as well as his brother, his father because he thought him unjust and his brother because he thought him selfish, immoral and a wastrel.

To Saul, whose life was a matter of daily moral striving to please God by unfaltering obedience to divine laws, the laxity of the father in not punishing the younger son was a disgrace. It was in the older brother that Saul with some satisfaction saw himself. He was not and he had never been like the prodigal son, distant from God and lost. In one corner of his mind, however, a voice reminded him of his times of despair with himself, when his inner contradictions were for him a barrier to God and made him feel a certain

alienation from God. The tiniest speck of doubt had entered
his consciousness. This doubt served as an irritant to increase
his fury against his captives. Luther translates Paul (Acts
26:10) to read "when they were killed, I expressed my
approval."

Others among the Galilean heretics (the word "Christian"
was not yet in use) dared to take their lives in their hands and
told their enraged captor, a parable that Jesus deliberately
aimed at blatant arrogance and self-righteousness.

According to this parable a Pharisee, one of Saul's con-
freres, appeared one day in the temple and, before God,
vaunted his superiority to all sinners. He boasted of his fast-
ing. He indulged in the absurdity of calling God's attention
to his personal generosity to God! Surely, none was to be
compared to him in obedience and righteousness.

At the same time a despised Roman agent, a tax collector,
entered the temple. He considered himself unworthy to draw
very near to the sanctuary. He hung back, beseeching God
to have mercy on him, a sinner. He gazed at the stone floor.
He would not lift up his eyes.

Jesus declared that it was this humble Jew, this Quisling,
who was forgiven and restored to God, not the Pharisee.

In Saul's eyes, these captives, wickedly misled by Jesus
were living in an upside down world. Who could be more
deserving of punishment than they? Not content to slander
the mainstay of true religion, the Pharisees, they maligned
the judgment of God. Yet had not something in him at times
prayed that prayer of the taxgatherer? "O God, have mercy
on me, sinner that I am. How can I ever know," he asked
himself, "whether I am good enough to please God by the
perfection of my obedience to his laws? Will I one day be like
that other rabbi who lay dying and tortured himself with the
question: 'Have I measured up? Have I made the grade?' "

Still other captives in Saul's charge were led by the Spirit
to tell him the parable of the landowner with the unusual,

to say the least, employment policy. A landowner hired workers for his vineyard, finding them when and where he could. He put some to work at daybreak, others at nine o'clock, still others at noon, at three o'clock, and even as late as an hour before sunset.

The landlord, out of kindness and perhaps because of the uniform needs of all the workers, paid them an identical, full day's wage.

Saul of Tarsus, in these three parables alone, had sufficient evidence against the disciples of Jesus. Here were heretics of the most subversive sort, with every word undermining Pharisaic orthodoxy. Saul also must have realized that the three parables were all saying the same thing: The God of the crucified Galilean is a God who values the person beyond all measure, far more than he values what the person achieves, and he will pay whatever price is necessary to share his bounty and offer his loving grace. The price was the father's agony of heart after his younger son ran away and was lost to him; the price was a full wage for the last minute labourer who came into the vineyard; the price was making up what was lacking in the publican, forgiving him and restoring him to himself.

Nor could Saul be unmindful that Jesus in his total self-giving death on the cross was making a final effort and sacrifice to make up what was lacking in the prodigal son, in the publican, and in the last man to come into the vineyard. The captives were bold to tell him so. He could not find it in himself altogether to deny it. If Jesus of Nazareth had died for them, why not for the elder brother, the Pharisee, and the full-time labourer in the vineyard?

Saul of Tarsus was already on the road to Damascus. Jesus was already more than he could face and stand down.

"Saul, Saul, why do you persecute me?" "Tell me, Lord, who are you?" "I am Jesus whom you are persecuting."

Son of Tarsus, the censorious older brother, became Paul

the Apostle, the younger son lived by faith and complete trust in the Father.

Saul of Tarsus, the Pharisee, became Paul the sinner, the tax collector who threw himself upon the mercy of God in grateful penitence.

Saul of Tarsus, the full-time deserving worker in the vineyard, became Paul the Apostle who knew that he came late to God's vineyard and yet, in God's eyes, was on the same footing as all the Apostles.

Paul the Apostle had heard the witness of the persecuted prisoners. They told him equally of Jesus' life, of his sayings, of his deeds on the one hand, and on the other hand, of his way of dying on the cross, that he had died in complete and utter trust in the Father. "Father, into thy hands I commend my spirit."

A whole new world and a whole new life exploded into view before his eyes. His old self, the old Saul, was overcome by the reckless love God manifested in the incarnation, the atonement, the resurrection and in the coming of the Holy Spirit. Henceforth he lived in the power of the cross and resurrection of Jesus. His life no longer centered in his moral striving but in his faith-union with Christ Jesus.

Just what does this mean: "His faith-union with Christ?" As Jesus placed himself unreservedly in the Father's hands in complete faith and self-surrender, so Paul in turn, and with unflinching devotion, placed his life and destiny in the hands of Jesus Christ his Saviour. This faith-union with Christ brought St. Paul the experience of being closer to God than he had ever been in his days as a Pharisee. Paul moved from a religion of the correct to a religion of the Christ.

The Reckless Love of God
(God the Justifier)

No one has ever "explained" the mystery of the cross, the mystery of its power to sustain and to heal. Indeed, Christians down the centuries have never been able to settle on a generally accepted doctrine of the atonement. When Jesus spoke of giving his life as "a ransom for many" (Matthew 20:28), was he not alluding to the kind of ransom which might be paid for the release of prisoners of war, or the freeing of all who have taken themselves into custody by their pride, their self-glorification, their self-idolatry, and all who are powerless to break free from themselves?

Likewise, when Paul says "you were bought with a price" (I Corinthians 6:20), is he not referring to the slave block and the setting free by the death of Christ of all who are in bondage to themselves, to self-glorification into which all have fallen? However, any interpretation which suggests that Christ died to appease an angry, vindictive God is in sharp conflict with the nature of God as revealed in Jesus.

Quite a different line of thought, and a more fruitful one, is suggested by the words of Paul: "God was in Christ reconciling the world to himself, not counting their trespasses against them" (II Corinthians 5:19). From the Godward side, the intent of the All-holy was clear. He sought to restore us, despite our sinfulness, to himself. From the manward side, Jesus was the representative of all men. Jesus was representative man. He overcame in man all selfish-assertiveness, all self-glorification, all self-worship. As representative man, Paul refers to Jesus as the second Adam. "The first Adam became a living being; the last Adam became a life-giving spirit" (I Corinthians 15:45).

> *"If He conquered as God, it profits us nothing; but if as man, we conquered in Him. For He is the second Adam sent from Heaven according to the Scriptures."*
> *(Cyril of Alexandria, A.D. 425)*

This is why Paul could say: "Thanks be to God who giveth us the victory through our Lord Jesus Christ" (I Corinthians 15:57).

The meaning of the cross is inexhaustible, whether we look at it from the Godward side or from the manward side. Maurice proclaimed that on the cross God was both the propitiator and the propitiated. There is a deep, instinctive longing in the human spirit to make expiation for wrong-doing. In Christ, God made expiation for us.

We may look more closely at the reckless nature of God's love, at the absolute scandal of the Gospel. The All-holy in the Person of his Son died on the cross so that, by a free act of grace to be received through faith, he might restore to himself and to his covenant:

> The sinner as a sinner,
> The egotist as an egotist,
> The hypocrite as a hypocrite,
> The seducer as a seducer,
> The killer as a killer,
> The hater as a hater,
> The adulterer as an adulterer,
> The whore as a whore,
> The cheat as a cheat,
> The failure as a failure,
> The hopeless one as a hopeless one,
> The depressed one as the depressed one.

Jesus picks us up where we are. Salvation and wholeness begin at that point where we decide to enter a faith-union with Christ. Christ has already established all the conditions which make a life of complete trust in God possible. He identified himself with us and died on the cross for us. He sent his Holy Spirit to be our ally and helper on our journey to wholeness.

He hates our sin but there can be no doubt whatsoever about his absolute love for us. There are no exceptions.

CHAPTER SIX

Dying-to-Live in Christ

God shows himself to us
Through lives that live for him.
                    Angus Dun

George Eliot in her novel *The Mill on the Floss* presents the reader with an unforgettable character sketch of the miller, Mr. Tulliver. "Mr. Tulliver regarded his rector with dutiful respect as he did everything else belonging to the Church but he considered that the Church was one thing and common sense another, and he wanted nobody to tell him what common sense was. Certain seeds which are required to find a nesting place for themselves under favorable circumstances have been supplied by nature with an apparatus of hooks, so that they will get a hold on their receptive surfaces. The spiritual seed which had been scattered over Mr. Tulliver had apparently been destitute of any corresponding provision and had slipped off to the winds again from a total absence of hooks."

A considerable array of useful hooks, cockleburs and Spanish needles confronts us as we now deal more directly with the subject of finding wholeness in Christ.

For all the jokes in these days about "born-again Christians," we were discussing this very subject in the last chapter. The subject is unavoidable, even assuming that it would be desirable to avoid it. Faith is experienced in two phases. In Phase One, God the Justifier delivers us into the new life of trust in him in which there is a conversion on the level of motivation. From a life of moral striving to make ourselves of some worth in our own eyes as well as in the eyes of God, we find a new life that is motivated by gratitude for our restoration to God, by grateful penitence. It is Eucharist (thanksgiving) that gives a name to our new motivation.

In Phase Two of the experience of faith, we take in hand what God has begun in us and, as co-workers with the Holy Spirit, we build on that. First we are "born" in Christ. Next, we "grow up" in Christ. It is in the "growing up" in Christ, that we come upon the array of useful hooks. The spiritual seed need not slip off to the winds as they did in the case of Mr. Tulliver.

Hook No. 1. Bind your aggression with love. We have noted that to admit to oneself the presence within oneself of angry, aggressive feelings is essential to one's wholeness. We have also acknowledged that immediately and angrily to act out the aggression, regardless of the circumstances, is one of the dubious axioms of "pop" psychology. Open rage and tantrums belong at best to three, four and five years of age before the human spirit is strong enough to preside over the interior components. A tantrum in a forty year old is rather ridiculous pyrotechnics.

To be sure, the energy mobilized by anger must find an outlet. Cushioned in as many comforts as we are and as crowded together in small living quarters as is often the case, ingenuity is sometimes required to find adequate means of draining away or defusing the anger. To pickaxe, dig and shovel the earth; to cut, saw, split, chisel or hammer nails into wood in a workshop; to swat at a volleyball, tennis ball or golf ball; to walk, jog or run are all excellent and one or another is possible for everyone. The oldest method of all is to walk it off. This is a most effective means because, before we had so many wheels, our legs were constantly in use. When anger flared and the adrenalin flowed, our legs churned whether in fight or in flight. Our legs even give us the impression of understanding what we are doing as we walk off our anger.

To bind your aggression with love will sound like a most unhealthy prescription to all who have succumbed to pop psychology or who have never looked into what it means to be an adult. Pop psychology turns things around. It gets things backward. Regression is not maturity. The language itself knows a lot. Look to the words: "To fly off the handle" is regression, not maturity. Consciously, to bind your aggression with love will not hurt you, and more to the point, you will not hurt anyone else.

Hook No. 2. Add renunciation to the inventory of your spirit. The word renunciation has all but disappeared from the vocabulary of this "all is permitted" age. Where sexuality is involved, the resolution of a conflict may well require a difficult and straightforward renunciation. We may toy with the idea of having our cake and eating it too. Reality separated us from the possibility of having our cake and eating it too when we were weaned from the breast in infancy.

In giving spiritual direction to ourselves and perhaps to others as well, we must reclaim from former ages two indispensable words: temptation and renunciation. If modern life has cast aside these words as old-fashioned, so much the worse for modern life as daily we are all discovering.

Hook No. 3. Never underestimate the power of your conscience. The persons who choose to read this book are not likely to be psychopaths, a psychopath being an individual devoid of conscience and destructively anti-social. A conscience does not have the power to make us happy but it decidedly has the power to make us unhappy. Someone who is experiencing serious self-dissatisfaction may not even recognize that self-dissatisfaction stems from a negative self-judgment, which is to say, from the conscience. On the level of conscience, self-dissatisfaction and guilt are interchangeable terms. Guilt can bring upon us a kind of sin sickness which needs attention, the attention of confession and forgiveness. Otherwise one may drift along in unhappiness and self-dissatisfaction. "Never underestimate the power of the conscience" is indeed a useful hook because guilt weakens the human spirit. The Holy Spirit is the ally and helper in lifting guilt from the human spirit and thereby restoring its strength.

Thus far in this chapter we have resumed our discussion of our inner components (earlier discussed in Chapter 3) in a new context, the new life in Christ. The Holy Spirit enables the human spirit more and more to bind its aggression with love and to utilize it creatively, to live into one's sexuality as a sacramental bond between two persons which transcends sex for self only, to respect and integrate the conscience which is not to be minimized by the human spirit. As instincts are to the animal, so conscience is to the human being. Take away the conscience from the human being and you have a second-rate candidate for the zoo. An animal's life is harmonized by its instincts. A human spirit, aided by the Holy Spirit and the conscience, must win through to its own harmony. Conscienceless, a human being's life is sheer chaos.

The Holy Spirit leads the human spirit more and more to die to selfish and destructive uses of aggression and sexuality, as well as to die to self-deception in relation to the conscience in order to live into a new self-image.

The Self-Image in the New Life

Hook No. 4. In the new life in Christ the self-image undergoes a more radical transformation than any of the interior components. As the self-image must be reshaped in adolescence, so it must be reshaped again as we "grow up in Christ." For the Holy Spirit now strives to restore the image of God in us. The mental picture we are given of ourselves is that of a person who is living one's way into creativity, freedom and love, the very same elements of the image of God in us. These capacities do not become new laws for us. They become new possibilities, fresh potentialities. They are forms, as it were, of being, living, and doing. Individuals, widely differing, will fill in and live out the forms in a rich variety of ways. However, to deny that we were born to be creative, loving and free is to abdicate as a human being.

The Holy Spirit will not lead us, in relation to our self-image, to live as though we were seeking to recover the lost good of our "pre-fall innocence." We shall never in this life be simply creative, loving and free. The old opposites in lesser strength will still be with us as long as we live. However, we accept them now with more tolerance of ourselves, with less fret and self-hatred and self-punishment. We die to the old pattern of living in the past and for the past in order to live toward the future and for the future. We trust in a deeper way and we risk in new ways as we lay claim to our essential selves, as we become what we are, spirits who have power over ourselves, are self-managing, self-directing. "Faith," says Kierkegaard, "awaits not proofs, but ventures," new ventures in creativity, freedom and love.

The Final Enemy of the Human Spirit

Hook No. 5. The human spirit, in the new life, is relieved

of the inordinate pride of self-sufficiency and decides for an absolute dependence upon God. We were made, and are made to be, creatures dependent upon God and trustful of him. A joyous alliance with the Holy Spirit brings a joyous reliance upon God.

Nonetheless, there is a certain undertow that marks your existence and mine, from start to finish, from birth to death, even from the new birth to our last day. The undertow to which I refer is the powerful inclination to relapse and to return to the religion of the natural man, to a legalism whereby we seek to earn a sense of worth before God, to earn our salvation.

Even before the writings of the New Testament were completed, this undertow was already operative in the primitive Church. Almost like a reflex, we turn back to legalistic Judaism. To this day the Church, in season and out, must swim against the ancient undertow. A communicant in Boston, on an Easter morning, proudly told me that by visiting many different Episcopal churches she had attended sixty Eucharists in the forty days of Lent. How ironic are Lenten good works when they are intended to make us worthy before God, or to make expiation to God when God in Christ, by his sacrifice on Good Friday and by his resurrection on Easter Sunday made the expiation for us and gave us a worth beyond all worths which are humanly derived.

The Gospel declares that God the Justifier has saved us to live in freedom, love and creativity by a divine grace that is received through faith. Beware of the all but indelible inclination to excise the heart of the Gospel. The name for this inclination to doubt the heart of the Gospel is sin. The opposite of sin is not virtue, not good works. The opposite of sin is faith. "Only believe and thou shalt live." The last hook is the major hook and, by far, the most useful; it is faith.

Part Four
Journey to Wholeness

CHAPTER SEVEN
Stages on the Journey Inward

Inward Journey and Outward Journey are familiar terms in our community. We use them to describe what the Christian life is all about. *

Elizabeth O'Connor

The pattern of the Christian life does indeed need to be redrawn more deliberately in terms of the inward journey and the outward journey. Both journeys are essential. Every day in the Christian life must include them both. Each feeds the other. Wholeness stems from the synergistic interplay of the two journeys.

Conversion is indeed a process. Very, very rarely is conversion a single event. When we undertake the two journeys, we are entering the conversion process. That is our objective on the road to wholeness: to enter and to participate in the conversion process.

An objective is to be distinguished from an outcome. What folly, for example, it is to make happiness an

---

*Elizabeth O'Connor, *Journey Inward, Journey Outward* (New York: Harper and Row, 1968), p. 10.

objective. As an objective, happiness eludes us. Happiness is an outcome, a by-product of seeking something else.

An anonymous Frenchman has unkindly remarked that America is the first nation in history to become decadent before it became mature. Whatever element of truth there may be in this statement is perhaps due to our trying to make happiness an objective.

In the strictest sense wholeness cannot be a direct objective. We approach or progress toward wholeness by participating in the conversion process. That is our clear and direct objective, participation in the conversion process. And there is something we can do about that. We can begin by embarking upon the journey inward. We can learn to pray. We can learn to pray by first being quiet before God.

Admittedly, one has to learn how to use silence. Being silent for any length of time seems not to come naturally to a twentieth century man or woman. At first try, being silent, alone with God and ourselves, may make us impatient, even uneasy.

Instead of giving up, we might stop and consider one or more of the following:

1. Think about the God into whose presence we have brought ourselves. For one thing he has you in particular, not just people in general, very much on his mind and heart.

2. In view of this fact we might follow the counsel of the Cure d'Ars: "Do not hesitate. Go straight to Him." Give up and give over to him all your moral striving for the time being.

3. Lay bare before God your spirit and your entire inner environment with all of its various components. Together with the Holy Spirit let your human spirit search out and examine those components, how you have deployed them and have or have not made a place for them in your life.

4. Empty your mind. To begin with, for only two or three minutes a day. Reject all thoughts which enter the mind. Lie fallow. Let the Holy Spirit ease the stress and tensions of your life. Let yourself fall through all of your ideas, notions, concepts of God and you will fall into God. He is beneath all mind-pictures of him.

5. Offer to God, if you can, a grateful heart. If for no readily conscious reason, then for this excellent reason. Thanks to God's revelation in Jesus Christ, we have been given a religion of having, not just a religion of seeking. Granted that much in vogue in recent years is a rejection of Christian answers as being of far less importance than asking appropriate and meaningful questions, nevertheless we do possess and can thank God for possessing a religion of having. We do have his love and forgiveness, our Lord Jesus Christ as a companion (com-pan = with bread) along the way, and we do have the gift of the Holy Spirit, the Lord and giver of life. The greatest of all gifts God has validated you in baptism and no person on earth can now or ever invalidate you. A person recovering from mental illness and a period of hospitalization said: "I feel invalidated and ashamed because I was mentally ill." Why? God has validated you, once and for all, now and forever. Only believe. Why is mental disease any more of a disgrace than a charley horse?

6. Use silence as a time to listen to God, to obey God. The word obey comes from the Latin *ob audire* which means to hear, to listen. To listen to God in silence restores our close personal touch with God.

7. In silence we learn to confess without using words and to be judged without hearing words. In silence the Holy Spirit finds us in our weakness and strengthens us in our impoverishment. In silence there comes the realization that he is present and that he is willing and able to help us. In

silence the Holy Spirit more often gives direction, not directions. Often the human spirit, strengthened by him, can take it from there.

In silence the goal is the orientation of your human spirit to the Holy Spirit.

8. Silence is also a time to listen to one's self while in the presence of God. "The most formidable enemy of the spiritual life (Ed., and of wholeness), and the last to be conquered is self-deception, and if there is a better cure for self-deception than silence, it has yet to be discovered."*

Finally, a time of daily silence enables us to commit to memory and to use the six prayer topics which matter most if we would participate in the conversion process and be made whole. To memorize these six topics is to have a prayer track, so that you may pray at any time, at any place and without additional aids. You may pray under one topic, or two or three, or all in a given time.

> Silence
> Simplicity
> Separateness
> Community
> Commitment
> Caring

The first three belong to the inward journey, the last three to the outward. However, all six topics need to be explored in the framework of prayer before the last three call us to action on the journey outward. With the practice of prayer now in mind, consider in turn each of the above.

Simplicity

The late bishop of Texas possessed many admirable qualities as well as a considerable dignity. He once lost his

---

*E. Herman, *Creative Prayer* (Cincinnati: Forward Movement Publications), p. 60.

way in the darkness of a university campus. "I can't see where I'm walking," complained the bishop. Right behind him in a sweet tone of voice, his wife made a practical suggestion. "Walk on the ground like the rest of us," she said.

It does bring a certain reassuring simplicity of spirit and of life when we walk on the ground. Especially is this true when we realize that the ground beneath our feet is God. Some of us have discovered that God, as the ground beneath our feet, does not give way even in the worst of times, whether of loss, isolation or dire illness. The ground does not quake or roll or break open into an abyss.

The obstacles to simplicity, both inner and outer obstacles, are numerous. There follows a digest of the most frequent obstacles. Of course all do not pertain to you. In a daily time of silence and prayer you may wish to ponder one or more obstacles which do stand in your way and, with the Holy Spirit as your ally and helper, deal with it or with them. None of these obstacles is in itself simple. Each is stubborn and tenacious when it is present to any significant degree. "This kind can come out only by prayer." And not in a single day.

1. Too much religion, or, better to say, a religion that is too complicated. In a day of criticism and analysis, we easily overlook the simplicity of Biblical religion. Deliverance and Covenant form the kernel of the Old Testament. Deliverance through Christ and a New Covenant of the Holy Spirit constitute the kernel of the New Testament.

In the District of Columbia, there is a beautiful contemporary house. In the center of that house there is a silo stairway, capped by a crystal clear dome. At night, when the lights in the house are turned out, one can stand at the bottom of that stairwell and, looking up, can see a window into the heavens and a multitude of stars, the handiwork of God. Jesus is for us such a window.

To change the metaphor, he is the One Center, the one focus. He makes possible for us a simplicity which would not otherwise be within our reach. If your religion seems to you overmuch and too complicated, look to him, to that One Center. All else is secondary.

2. Perfectionism deprives us of simplicity in outlook and spirit. That moral perfectionism should be an obstacle to simplicity for so many Americans is no surprise when we consider even briefly the history of morals in our country.

> 17th Century: Character, duty, principles
> 18th Century: Honesty, industry, frugality
> 19th Century: Decency, respectability, success
> 20th Century: Comfort, wealth, status

Indeed, what a staggering accumulation of heavy scruples and of goals both worthy and dubious. You will note that as the centuries have passed, we have moved from inner realities to external ones more and more. Alas, we have lengthened the distance from our indigenous selves as we have followed the American way. Our values need sorting out, to say the least. Simplicity becomes difficult when there is enslavement to layer upon layer of goals. Do you live under the weight of many moralistic layers? Do you live under the lash of many "oughts"?

3. Procrastination (meaning literally "wait until tomorrow") becomes an obstacle often born of perfectionism and too much religion. We back away from it all and have a good old-fashioned sit down strike. However, procrastination brings you to a point of necessity where you must fly into a frenzy of work which impresses no one except perhaps yourself, and is utterly exhausting. Thomas Aquinas writes that "Peace is the tranquility of order." We may alter this saying to read "Simplicity is the tranquility of

order." We take time in silence and prayer to order our inner and outer lives. How often we find ourselves putting our desk in order, or our bureau, or washing the car thoroughly, in and out. Does this attainment of limited order in a restricted area of our outer lives give us the illusion of working through to some inner order and simplicity?

4. "All or none" syndrome. Do you remember at three or four years of age when, if you could not have the whole cupcake, you would have none of it? A little four year old, Gill, was offered half a cookie by her mother. Gill knew the other half was for her brother. She held up her hand before her mother, spacing her thumb and forefinger one-eighth of an inch apart, and said: "Mother, I love you this much!"

We carry over into adult life this all or none attitude. We will find it present within us, sometimes grossly, sometimes ever so subtly. For you is this attitude an obstacle to simplicity?

5. "I am pegged to the wall" assumption. A desultory idea that operates deep and powerfully in the emotional life of many persons goes with the saying: "I cannot help being what I am or how I am." This false notion can discourage us utterly from trying to intervene in our lives and bring some order and discipline into them. Discipline can be defined in precisely these terms. Discipline is actively and intentionally intervening in your own life for the purpose of bringing order and simplicity into your existence. Why are you, why is your spirit, so passive in relationship to your own life? After all, you can be assertive without being selfishly assertive.

6. Fear of weakness and inadequacy. We can expend enormous energy fighting fear of weakness, inadequacy and failure. Some persons fight their fear better when they keep it secret. Other persons make better soldiers when they can

talk about their fear. In any case, anxious preoccupation with one's fear can rob us of simplicity of spirit.

As in times of dryness of spirit, so in times of anxiety and weakness of spirit, we have recourse to silence and to the near presence of the Holy Spirit. To be thus "poor in spirit" is by no means to be defeated in spirit. Hope, confidence and the courage of faith (even boldness in the Lord), are among the primary God-given possessions of the believing spirit. In silence think on these things, not once but many times and, if necessary, through many days. In simplicity and with a courage that dares and risks, act as though it is impossible to fail. Let this be your watchword. Act as though it is impossible to fail. You may be surprised at the outcome, however much your anxiety may quite literally be making you shake and tremble at a given but feared task.

Separateness

How disturbing it is to be confronted with the question: "Have you ever chosen separateness?" Of course you are a separate individual, one of a kind, different from all persons who ever lived, a duplicate of no forerunner in a million years, never to be reduplicated in another million years, if we may judge from the past. Cloning is at the talking, not the walking, stage. If ever there is a clone, it will differ from the original by being a carbon copy and not the royal ribbon edition.

We may let these very words bounce off of us because they arouse the anxiety of separateness, solitariness, aloneness. A kind of cosmic anxiety. We may not allow ourselves to recognize this obvious fact of our separateness. Far harder is allowing ourselves not just to recognize but to realize our separateness, our uniqueness and our ultimate aloneness. To let that fact "sink in" brings some thoughtful persons to the edge of panic. They hasten to reject the thought, push it aside and resume the safety of losing their individuality in the crowd. Kierkegaard experienced a love-hate relationship with his own separateness and uniqueness. To be sure, he championed uniqueness and at the same time he experienced a dread and anxiety because he was different from all others, just as we all are.

I have deliberately and purposely chosen the word separateness as a station on our prayer track. Sin is willful separation from God, neighbor and self. Separateness is simply a given in human existence, namely, the particularity of the individual. To own our singularity in all of our finiteness and weakness drives us toward God, not away from him. Separation is alienation from God, neighbor and self. Separateness is a door which opens onto solidarity with God, neighbor and self. Acknowledging and affirming our separateness is a vitally necessary prelude to every one of the succeeding stages: to community, to commitment and to caring.

God save us from a religious system or a cookie cutter Christianity which fails to acknowledge not only the uniqueness of every individual but the uniqueness of every individual's relationship to God.

CHAPTER EIGHT

Stages on the Outward Journey

*For all mortals their own self-awareness is
their God.*
                    Menander (c. 350 B.C.)

Community

Immediately following the discussion of separateness in the preceding chapter, an equal emphasis must now be placed upon community. As surely as he came to bring wholeness to the individual Jesus came to found a new faith-community.

The first step in the outward journey is to take your place in a faith-community. Your community is an appropriate subject for your prayers. Again let me state that all six topics, those of the last chapter and those of this chapter have their rightful places in our times of silence and prayer. Scan the list once more:

> Silence
> Simplicity
> Separateness
> Community
> Commitment
> Caring

Your faith-community needs your presence at public worship but, equally, your private prayers.

The spiritual impact of a congregation upon its neighborhood and upon the world stems from the prayer life of its individual members. A personal prayer life is the lost dimension of the contemporary church. In three generations we have drifted away from daily private prayer. We have increasingly placed almost the entire burden of the church's prayer life on public worship, or, in the liturgical churches, upon the Eucharist. Yet the power of the Eucharist comes fully to life only when it is faith speaking to faith, that is, to the individually nurtured faith of the several members or communicants.

We do not go to the communion rail to find faith. We go to him in his living presence to offer him our believing, thankful lives. The Eucharist has genuine sacramental power only for an already existing and nurtured personal faith or very little may be expected to happen, except perhaps a rich aesthetic experience.

We first pray for our faith-community that we may upbuild the Body of Christ and then we have a corporate base (1) for extending the mission of God's church and (2) we have a supportive and nurturing community to do our own appointed work in the world in his name.

First, consider the most obvious (and nowadays the most frequently evaded) task of the church, namely, its mission to the people of the world. The world around. Why missions? Why not a closed shop, all for ourselves? Why not an inhouse program and nothing more?

God becomes a bit stubborn, awkward and inconvenient at this point.

There is a very real bond between Christ and every individual on this earth. For no one stands outside the circle of his concern or can step beyond the reach of his arms outstretched on the cross. The Word made flesh is addressed to all who hear and respond, to all who hear and reject and to all who have never even heard. Christ died for all the peoples of the world.

Since not all persons respond to God's overtures, we are commissioned to be his hands, his voice and his body. We are to speak his word and to do his will. The Christian mission today takes, and must take many forms and undertake many diverse tasks.

Task-oriented mission groups after the manner of those at work in The Church of the Saviour, Washington, D.C., are exportable to other churches, and perhaps to yours, when adapted to local conditions. They can at least serve as signposts for your own faith community. Books on the mission structures of this unusual church are found at the back of this book.

Many persons in the Church today are increasingly understanding their life and work in the world as a mission and ministry given them by God. Their faith communities offer a source of strength for their tasks in the home, in the professional world, in offices, on farms, in government.

To have a base in a faith community can indeed help us to overcome fragmentation and scatteredness of spirit.

Commitment

The Bible proclaims the absolute majesty and magnitude of God. He is the totality who is above all and in all, before all history and beyond all history, a presence both above us and in us. Rufus Jones referred to him as the "Beyond who is within."

The Bible discloses a God who commands all creation and all creatures, including ourselves. He commands but does not coerce our total allegiance and our total continuing fidelity. Among all creatures only we can say "yes" or "no" to him. All other creatures move in a marvelous harmony under a natural system of instincts which compel them. "God is a spirit and those who worship him must worship him in spirit and in truth" (John 4:23). The human spirit can make choices. One may definitely and with finality decide for God.

Faith is an act, a decision as well as being a gift of God. For some of us at least to make the decision of faith, or the act of commitment, is not experienced as an act of iron will as much as it is a yielding of the heart to a power that is greater than ours and which we have first come to know in Jesus Christ through the Holy Spirit.

Commitment, whether as an inspired act of will or as a spirit-led yielding of the heart to God is the portal whereby we finally enter the conversion process which alone can bring us to wholeness.

Maurice wrote that: "We dwell in a twilight of half-realized truths, half-followed convictions." A definite, reflective, adult commitment can take us out of that twilight into the bright light of day. There is no doubt in my mind whatever that the first meaning of Christianity is personal commitment to our Lord Jesus Christ, to the God he reveals and to the Holy Spirit of Pentecost.

Persons whose experience with religion has been negative and who are skittish about "surrendering" or who fear an overridden and diminished self (actually grace enhances, enriches selfhood, not the reverse) may follow a somewhat different route. Religiously skittish people have followed Samuel Taylor Coleridge by practicing a "suspension of disbelief." If you are such a person, your first step in commitment may be to suspend your doubt and disbelief; do not deceive yourself by falsely disclaiming your doubts but by simply setting them aside. If suspending your disbelief for a time is all that you can honestly do, never mind. Go with that and be open to what is to follow. By an increasing effort on your part to learn of Christ and through Christ, discover who he is reported to have been, in his humanity. As you read the scriptural accounts, you may be amazed to learn how much like you he is in his humanity, in his times of need, in his loneliness, in his evident need of friends and of support and help. You may go on to discover that the more you know of him, the more you sense that he is different, that he has truly been given a divine mission, that he pursued that mission with a sacrificial self-giving that can only be designated as divine in nature and a revelation of his own divine nature.

Persons who have followed this route of suspended disbelief, often go through two stages on the way to commitment. In the first stage, working with Scripture, they have glimpses of recognition that he is truly human and that his humanity is surpassed by something else. In the second stage of their growth they move from recognizing the truth about Jesus Christ to a deep realization that he is truly the Son of God. When this happens, they are already in the circle of believers. Their commitment is experienced as a yielding of their hearts to him. So, after all, if you are such a person and follow this path of suspended disbelief for a time, you will have discovered that you do not have to swallow hard, blink, and say, "Yes, I believe if I must."

Aspects of Commitment

1. We must affirm and reaffirm our commitments. Whether our commitment begins with a leap of faith or with a suspension of disbelief, when that commitment is finally made, we must recognize a necessity which is due to our weakness. Commitment to Christ is not something done once and for all, something to which we never need return to give further attention. Quite the contrary, ever and again we find that we must reflect upon, accept afresh and reaffirm our commitment. I confess to my own need in this

respect. In the years of my ordained ministry I have set aside some time on Labor Day weekend in September (why do we exclude Labor Day from the Church year?) to recommit myself to my ordination and to the deeper purposes of my ministry as a dean and teacher in a theological seminary, whether with trustees, faculty or with my students. How else than by accepting and reaccepting our commitments can we remain steadfast in our spirits?

2. Commitment is to a life of detached-attachment. As we have noted more than once, our faith tells us that there is another order. Our lives as Christians are rooted and grounded in that other order. Our ultimate attachment is to the divine order that is other than this visible world. In this world we, therefore, have the freedom to sit loosely to all the pressing proximities of worry, daily strivings to meet routine needs, to sickness and disabilities. Jesus tried to indicate this type of detachment when he told us to consider the lilies of the field, how "they toil not, neither do they spin." We Christians are in this world but are not of this world. We are not intended for a life of frenzied, relentless striving. We are to be steadfast and to do things in their season. We need not to be caught up in a frantic pace. Manic dashing about is not a Christian obligation. Detached-attachment as a way of life should frequently be the subject of our reflective prayers and might well find a place in our journal where we bring it under review from time to time. Known so well by Christians who preceded us in generations gone by, in much contemporary Christianity, living in a spirit of detached-attachment is a lost secret.

3. Commitment involves daily disciplines. A person who sought to bring a small group in his faith-community to adopt a schedule of daily disciplines was given the impression that the members of the group really wanted spirituality without discipline. In practice a committed Christian might well move gradually toward twenty

minutes a day reading the Scriptures experientially. Such reading is not the same as devoting oneself to a commentary about a passage in the Bible and remaining solely on the intellectual, impersonal plane, as one examines a book review. To read the Scripture experientially is constantly to ask oneself: "What is the Holy Spirit saying to me in this passage?" To ask also what you will do about your finding, how you will alter your life and conduct? Such daily disciplines may have a place for quiet, for emptying the mind (only one or two minutes a day to begin with), for reflective prayer which I believe is the most needed kind of prayer in the modern world. People do not take time to think in these days. Of course our prayers of intercession for those we love and for others whose needs we also know, for peace and justice in the world, jobs for the poor and food for the hungry, and help for the suffering and companionship for the dying, belong to our commitment.

Many persons have found that keeping a journal is a valuable discipline for the following reasons:

a. In relation to the use of Scripture: After reading a passage, to "articulate" with a pen what you believe the Holy Spirit is saying to you in that passage helps to drive the message home.

b. In relation to every station on your prayer track: Your thoughts on silence, simplicity, separateness, on community, commitment, caring, when written in your journal are likely to lead you into ever more meaningful understanding of God, of your family and neighbors, and of yourself.

c. In relation to continuity in your devotions: To look back now and then, what you wrote six months ago, or a year or five years ago will either encourage you by showing how you have inwardly grown or spur you on if you have become lax.

4. Commitment bears fruit in a mission, that is, in a task to and for the community. Prayer precedes fruitful action as surely as thought is intended to precede action.

Faith, like commitment, is a movement of the will to negate the self-focussed will and to release the pneumatic will, that is, the spirit-led will.

And this brings us to the subject of caring.

Caring

Biblical religion presents us with the difficult task of discovering what the Scripture means by the term love. Even more difficult is our coming into possession of a loving heart.

Recall again the distinction we are making between objectives and outcomes. Love in the Biblical sense is to be radically distinguished from all topics in this chapter which we thus far have considered. To some extent we can take the initiative in our times of prayer and actively invoke in ourselves silence, simplicity, a realization of separateness, the resolve to find and participate in a faith-community. We can even take ourselves kicking and screaming into a period of silence because previously we have decided upon such a discipline, and we can gradually grow inwardly quiet, centering down into simplicity of spirit, courageously accepting the stark fact of our separateness and ultimate aloneness.

We cannot, however, absolutely cannot will to love or will to have a loving heart, and, lo, there it is. The first five of our topics are chiefly objectives and only in a minor sense are they outcomes as compared with love and caring. A loving heart is truly an outcome of something else. The words of John Coburn can be directly applied here: "Attend God and he will get his work done." Attend God by prayerfully giving yourself to the search for God, to being

with him, to listening to him. God will then get his work
done; he will create in you a new heart and a fresh
compassion. A spirit-led loving heart is the aim and end of
the conversion process.

Meaning of Love in the Biblical Sense

1. The Love of God. The love of God, or love in the heart
of God, motivated his creation of the world and of
ourselves. The love of God underlies both the Old
Testament Covenant and the New Testament Covenant.
The love of God sent his Son into the world. It was the
divine love which was expressed on the cross and in the self-
giving of the divine Son.

The love of God raised up the prophets, called the
disciples and the apostles, and he continues to call people to
be his ministers. He calls you. The love of God is the decisive
reality in the world and in your life, for he includes you in
that love.

To you, to the human spirit at the core of your being, the
love of God sends his Holy Spirit to be your Inner Teacher,
your Inner Light.

Loving hearts cannot be mass produced. They must be
"hand-made" and hand-tooled by the power of the Holy
Spirit who in the conversion process reshapes what is there.
The Holy Spirit is indeed the Lord and Giver of life and the
Maker of the loving heart. The Holy Spirit impels us to love
but he does not compel us. At times he floods our hearts
with a spontaneous feeling which propels us to the side of
our neighbor who is in need.

2. Love for God. Catherine of Siena puts these words into
the mouth of God:

> *God speaks and says: "I require that you
> should love me with the same love with
> which I love you. This indeed you cannot*

> *do because I loved you without being loved*
> *. . . You cannot repay the love which I*
> *require of you, and so I have placed you in*
> *the midst of your fellows, that you may be*
> *to them that which you cannot be to me,*
> *that is to say, that you love your neighbor*
> *of free grace without expecting any return*
> *from him, and what you do to him I count*
> *as done to me . . . This love must be sincere*
> *because it is with the same love with which*
> *you love me, that you must love your*
> *neighbor."*

Christian love is loving back to God who first loved us, who came to our side in Christ and who died for us. He wanted to win us, not force us; to deal with our spirits as kindred spirits that our relation, let me say once again, may be Spirit to spirit, Person to person.

The love for God is indeed to be expressed by loving our neighbor and especially our neighbor in need.

Conclusion of this Chapter

We have delineated in this chapter a prayer track. That track leads us, with others in our faith-community, perhaps a small nurturing group within that community, to name a task and to form our life around that task, supporting each other, praying with and for each other at regular times and providing sufficient time.

During certain periods in an individual's life his call may not be to participate in such a task force but rather to understand his ministry as parent and provider. After all, both fathers and mothers are parents and providers who meet family needs. They are, in fact, ministers.

At any rate, to be a Christian in the world, to be whole, to be fully human, fully alive will produce needs also in ourselves. Where will we get the strength and the resources to follow God's will for us?

Gifts and the Will of God for Us

People often ask, sometimes in frustration: "How can I possibly know the will of God for me?" I do not believe that the answer to this question is as vague as some people might like it to be, or as hidden theologically as others would like it to be. God has endowed us with certain gifts. When we dedicate those gifts to him, when we live our way into them and exercise them, we are both following the will of God which has been written out for us in our natures in terms of our gifts and we are finding personal fulfillment and wholeness.

It is not always easy to know one's gifts or to believe that they are present and are significant. Here is where the fellowship of the Holy Spirit, the faith-community, the Church, has a ministry for us and to us. By receiving help in identifying our gifts, the ministry of others prepares us for our own ministry. Thus a mutual support group can assist in clarifying God's will for us.

Now we move on to consider the sources of courage available to us on our journey to wholeness.

CHAPTER NINE

Courage for the Journey to Wholeness

To own and confess is Life,
To deny and disown is Death.
J. T.

Courage and Repentance

Repentance is the key to the courage which enables us to persist in our search for wholeness.

Unfortunately the meaning of the word repentance has become elusive. Nonstop, though of course necessary, the pulpit use has rounded this word into a slippery stone which slides harmlessly from the pulpit to the floor, eluding all ears. We must take in hand mallet and chisel. We must, like sculptors, let the meaning that is there in the stone find outline and shape once more. Our wholeness depends upon our understanding the meaning of repentance.

To repent, or repentance, means to choose oneself absolutely, that is, to choose the self in its entirety. As we have seen, "oneself" is an admixture of good and evil. Our essential self, that is, our creativity, our freedom, our

73

capacity to love, is homogenized with the opposite of
ourselves, with our fallen selves, that is, with our demonic
destructivity, with our self-serving license, and with our
self-glorification.

Our personal centers as well as every one of the interior
components of our personalities have been affected by the
Fall. There is no wholeness in us.

To stand before God admitting ourselves to be all that we
are, withholding nothing, hiding nothing, confessing the
demons and the darkness within ourselves as well as the
God-given light that is in us. Thus to make every effort to be
honest before God is, by the very experience of the act, to
feel repentant, it is to know the sorrow of repentance. It is
decidedly not enough to understand repentance to mean a
passive and resigned mood of saying, "I'm sorry because I'm
sorry because I'm sorry," as pietism would have us to say
and supposedly to be content.

Rather we must do a very difficult thing in the midst of
our sorrow of repentance. We must choose ourselves as we
are. We must choose absolutely the sinful conglomeration of
our conflicted beings, omitting nothing. Before God to
choose oneself in this total way is precisely the same as
repenting oneself. In the act of repentance, we cannot let go
of even the meanest and most despicable quality in oneself.
We cannot deny or disown even the most shameful and
guilt-ridden deed of past or present.

As God forgives all that we are and all that is within us, so
he holds us accountable for all that we are and for all that is
in us. In what I am writing here I owe a large debt to Søren
Kierkegaard, as you will discover when you read the
appendix to this book. What you will find there, thought-
fully read, has been and is of immense value to his many
students and readers.

To "choose oneself" does not mean to "prefer oneself" or
to "approve oneself" or simply "to accept oneself." To

accept ourselves with all of our faults is a psychologically healthy thing to do. Such self-acceptance, however, can be done in a spirit of resignation and passivity. On the other hand, to choose oneself absolutely, actively and positively, to choose oneself before God is far more difficult; it is far more than a psychological transaction with oneself. It is repentance before God. It is total accountability to God.

The alternatives to choosing oneself are not inviting: to deny parts of oneself, or to disown ugly aspects of oneself. To reject oneself before God is a blasphemous denial of all that he has done to save us and to make us whole. Every pastor knows how many persons come for help in dealing with their self-hatreds and their self-rejections and how far they are, and we are, from repentance, from owning ourselves completely and choosing ourselves in toto.

To repent is to find a new measure of courage and wholeness.

Courage and the Eucharist

The power of the Eucharist as a source of courage will be explained here in relation to various ways in which the need for wholeness finds expression, as set forth in the Preface of this book.

Consider first, however, that in the Eucharist the priest does not by some magic of conjuration or incantation bring down to the altar the presence of Christ. Rather in this sacrament Christ calls us ever and again to his side to refresh and renew our faith-union with him. Times of fragmentation and scatteredness, of confusion in our beliefs and of self-dissatisfaction are never dealt with once and for all, to be over and done with. Valleys and mountain tops are the contours of life. By repeatedly returning to Christ in the Lord's Supper or the Mass, in the Eucharist or the Holy Communion, regardless of the name we customarily give the sacrament, our need for courage and wholeness is met.

1. "I feel so disordered at the center of my being." We have examined our inner components, our conscience and self-image, our sexuality and our aggression. We have seen how confusion may arise in regard to any one of them and how conflicts may arise among them. We have noted how our essential natures decree that we are to be creative, free and loving and yet how we habitually fall into our opposites. We have discovered that our human spirits must rely on the Holy Spirit to make self-mastery possible. At the same time our natural bent is to try to go it alone without God. Is it so surprising that a person feels disordered at the center of his or her being?

Recall that our personhood finds its center in our human spirit. Our human spirit finds its center in the Holy Spirit. In the Eucharist the Holy Spirit comes from Christ to empower and enable the human spirit to gain self-mastery and to bring order out of disorder. This new life brings new courage.

2. "I feel so scattered and my life seems so scattered." A devastating sense of scatteredness comes from our goals which, when they go unexamined, tend to multiply beyond our ability to manage. At the Eucharist the Holy Spirit intervenes, breaks into our fragmentations, to ask: Where are you going? What are you doing? And why? Often it is in the Eucharist that we are given an agenda for our daily meditations which are to follow. Thus, actually to be doing something about our scatteredness awakens courage.

3. "I think things would be better with me if I knew what to believe." Recall Maurice's reminder that, "we live in a twilight of half-realized truths, and of half-followed convictions." Recall also the basic simplicity of Biblical religion. Deliverance and the Covenant are the heart of the

Old Testament. Deliverance in Christ and a New Covenant in him are the heart of the New Testament.

The Eucharist is a re-presentation of our deliverance by the Cross and the Resurrection, and of the establishment by the Holy Spirit of the New Covenant in Christ. In the Eucharist we are made participants and sharers in Christ's death and resurrection. Moreover, time and again we are reinstated in the New Covenant. The Eucharist offers the best possible context in which our half-realized truths may become fully and deeply realized and where our half-followed convictions may be consummated. Courage grows as convictions are implemented.

4. "I am carrying around a great burden of self-dissatisfaction." As we have already noted, self-dissatisfaction stems from a negative self-judgment and is simply another name for guilt. Many self-dissatisfied, unhappy people are not aware that guilt is their problem, or that religion is relevant to their problem. The Eucharist is where we go to undertake the hard task of choosing ourselves as guilty and where we confess and are forgiven. God here offers us three closely linked gifts: forgiveness, enhanced freedom which comes from a sense of being forgiven and courage which comes from the greater freedom.

5. "I am too self-focussed. Somehow, and I don't know how, I need to break free from myself." The Eucharist directly challenges the self-focussed person. The sacrament is an individual act but basically it is a corporate act. Christ who is King and Head of every man is first of all the King and Head of his Church, a corporate body.

In the New Testament that which is considered of supreme worth is not the individual person as this age prefers to believe. Of supreme worth in the New Testament is love and love immediately indicates the corporate nature of Christianity. To love one's neighbor, there must be a neighbor.

If Christ in the Eucharist is allowed really to enter our individual lives, and our corporate life as a faith-community, we are sent on mission. We are sent on the King's business. Our lives become neighbor-focussed, mission-focussed, Lord- and King-focussed, less and less self-focussed. The growing freedom from self feeds a growing courage.

CHAPTER TEN

Wholeness may be Yours

In the opening lines of this book we observed how commonly people are ambivalent about wholeness, about really being at their best, full of hope and health, and fully alive. A zest for life is only possible when there is in the person a sense of genuine freedom.

Is it freedom that makes us uneasy? Recall Kierkegaard's statement that "anxiety is the dizziness of freedom." Are we not, at least at times, afraid of our own feelings? Usually hidden in the nooks and crannies of our beings, we may nevertheless know that there are present in us dangerous wishes and impulses. Throw caution to the wind and dismember that petty neighbor next door with your gossip? Is that perhaps your wish?

Gossip, by the way, is a truly fallen term, coming as it does, from the old English "God's sib" which meant godmother. In "olden times," godmothers were constantly in and out of the nearby homes of their godchildren. They knew enough about their families to slaughter any member of the family with their tongues. The term "God's sib" deteriorated into gossip for obvious reasons. Tongues can lacerate. Gossip can destroy. Robust health makes for a robust tongue. A contemporary person may want the safety of a dampening half-health, so that a mean wag can only half wag.

Again, a man who fantasizes about giving his boss a prehistoric hole in the head, may debilitate his right arm by placing his elbow on a bar too often and too long at a time, or by overeating, oversmoking and overworking. He thereby manages to take himself into his own custody for safekeeping, into the custody of his chronic fatigue.

Still another person, man or woman, reaches age forty or thereabouts. He or she experiences what the Germans call "the panic of the closing doors." Life's chances seem to be running out. The monotony of conjugality, to use a less than euphonious phrase, has set in. Alas, the same torso and the same two legs over and over again. The temptation for a man to run around the town while there is yet time, or for a woman to sleep around the block before her beauty fades is real and constitutes a dangerous threat to a substantial conscience. Better to hang back from becoming free and fully alive. To be sure, vast numbers of the "liberated" run and swing but seldom do they claim a greater zest for life as their reward. Martinis may take the conscience out of the picture but alcohol, otherwise, brings diminishing returns and sometimes, alas, no returns at all.

How very often anxiety and semi-health are, in fact, the dizziness of freedom. After all, wholeness means wholeness. Components of the inner environment are all members of one whole. Aggression cannot say to the conscience "I have no need of thee." Sexuality cannot say to the self-image "I have no need of thee." The human spirit cannot say to any one of them "I have no need of thee."

Every individual component needs more than all else the human spirit, in place and functioning as the governor and integrator of all the components. The human spirit needs above all else the Holy Spirit. The fear of freedom diminishes as the human spirit is aligned or realigned with the Holy Spirit, and as repentance and accountability are taken seriously.

Wholeness may be yours by daring to live in the power of the Cross. Among the Jews of central Europe in Hitler's day was a remarkable young man named Paul-Louis Landsberg. Landsberg was born in Bonn, the son of a professor of law. A brilliant, careful thinker, he became a professor of philosophy at the age of twenty-five. In 1933, he and his wife fled from the Nazis to Spain. With the coming of the revolution in Spain, they fled to Paris. After France was occupied by the Germans in 1940, Landsberg and his wife were placed in separate concentration camps. She suffered an emotional collapse and was hospitalized. He escaped from his camp to search for her. He was arrested by the Gestapo and died in a concentration camp near Berlin in 1943 at the age of forty-two.

For some years he had been drawn to Christian thought and Catholic practice although he never became a member of the Church. After Hitler came to power, Landsberg thought and wrote in circumstances which made it all too clear that there are times when it is easier to die than to live. Quite understandably, something in him wanted to throw in the sponge, to quit life and suffering. Something else in him wanted to find sufficient support, sufficient grace, to live. "All knowledge is belief," he said, "and belief demands something beyond itself. . . ."* Under the pressure of personal need but with continuing scholarly care, he drew nearer to the Christian faith in his last years. He wrote several poems "To Christ" in which he calls Christ "the dearest light of my soul."

From 1930 on, he carried poison with him. Shortly before his arrest at Pau in 1943 he wrote to a friend: "I have now

---

*Paul-Louis Landsberg, *The Experience of Death and the Moral Problem of Suicide* (New York: Philosophical Library, 1953), p. xii.

met Christ—He has revealed Himself to me." When seized by the Gestapo, he placed his dependence on his Christ. He discarded the poison. The figure on the cross made it possible for Landsberg to say to himself: "Don't throw away your cross!" A fellow prisoner declared that Landsberg in his last days did not for a moment abandon determination, goodness and faith.

To love is to suffer. If we are caring persons, we have suffered, or we are suffering, or we will suffer. On our journey to wholeness we shall most certainly know both joy and suffering. Joy carries us but we must carry suffering. We must carry the cross.

On the road to Calvary, Simon of Cyrene for part of the way carried the cross for Jesus. Simon is the image of every one of us when he or she is carrying a cross. We walk behind Jesus, as Simon did. We need only look ahead; we see him. We take courage. God's keeping power becomes our staying power.

Wholeness may be yours by daring to live in the power of the Resurrection. In part our staying power comes also from the known future into which Jesus is entering as he moves towards his death, namely, his Resurrection. We also have a known destiny. His Resurrection is an assurance of our own. His Resurrection means, for us now, no less than the power of hope, love, joy and peace.

To participate ever more fully in the conversion process as you travel your inward and outward journeys is your clear objective. Your wholeness is the sure and certain outcome.

EPILOGUE

There is another order
Textured of cosmic cross
And eternal victory

He who drops his anchor there
Is set free and given power
In this present order

To appropriate wholeness
To be 'fully human, fully alive'

Bold in the Lord
Fearing nothing.

To Choose Oneself Absolutely Is To Repent
Søren Kierkegaard*

"I cannot often enough repeat the proposition, however simple it may be in itself, that choosing oneself is identical with repenting oneself. For upon this everything turns."

"Even the richest personality is nothing before he has chosen himself, and on the other hand even when one might be called the poorest personality he is everything when he has chosen himself; for the great thing is not to be this or that but to be oneself, and this everyone can be if he wills."

"He (who) has not chosen himself absolutely . . . is not in any free relation to God, and precisely in freedom consists the characteristic Christian piety."

"The man we are speaking of discovers that the self he chooses contains an endless multiplicity . . . Therefore, it requires courage for a man to choose himself. When the passion of freedom is aroused in him (and it is aroused by the choice, as also it is presupposed in the choice) he chooses himself and fights for the possession of this object as he would his eternal blessedness; and it is his eternal blessedness. He cannot relinquish anything in this whole, not the most

*Søren Kierkegaard, *Either/Or*, trans. David F. Swenson and Lillian Marvin Swenson. Copyright 1944 © 1971 by Princeton University Press. Excerpts from pp. 150-216 reprinted by permission of Princeton University Press.

painful, not the hardest to bear, and yet the expression for this fight, for this acquisition is . . . *repentance*. He repents himself back into himself, back into his family, back into the race, until he finds himself in God. Only on these terms can he choose himself, and he wants no other terms, for only thus can he absolutely choose himself."

"As soon as I love freely and love God I repent. And if there might be any other reason why the expression for my love of God is repentance, it would be because He has loved me first. And yet this is an imperfect account of the reason, for only *when I choose myself as guilty do I choose myself absolutely*, if my absolute choice of myself is to be made in such a way that it is not identical with creating myself; and though it were the iniquity of the father which passed by inheritance to the son, he repents of this as well, for only thus can he choose himself, choose himself absolutely; and though tears were to blot out everything, he holds on to repentance, for only thus can he choose himself. His self is, as it were outside of himself, and it has to be acquired, and repentance is his love for this self, because he chooses it absolutely out of the hand of the eternal God."

"For I know only one sorrow which could bring me to despair and with that hurl all things down, the sorrow of discovering that repentance was a delusion, not a delusion with respect to forgiveness but with respect to the accountability forgiveness implies."

"Only when in his choice a man has assured himself, is clad in himself, has so totally penetrated himself that every moment is attended by the consciousness of a responsibility for himself . . . only then has he repented himself, only then is he concrete."

"He who chooses himself . . . has himself as his task."

SUGGESTED READING
On Finding Your Way

Books by Elizabeth O'Connor:

Journey Inward, Journey Outward. Harper and Row. New York. 1975 Paperback.

Eighth Day of Creation. Word Books. 1971.

Our Many Selves. Harper and Row. New York. 1970. Paperback.

* * * * *

Poverty of Spirit. J. B. Metz. Newman Press. New York. 1968.

How People Change. Allen Wheelis. Harper and Row. New York. 1975. Paperback.

For Meditation and Prayer

Creative Prayer. E. Herman. Forward Movement Publications. 412 Sycamore St., Cincinnati, Ohio 45202. Paperback.

A Book of Hours. Elizabeth Yates. The Seabury Press. New York. 1976.

Your Word is Near. Huub Oosterhuis. Paulist Press. New York. 1968. Paperback.

New Seeds of Contemplation. Thomas Merton. New Directions Co. Paperback.